EASY GUITAR WITH RIFFS AND SOLOS

# PINK
# FLOYD

Cover Photo: Jeffrey Mayer / atlasicons.com

ISBN 978-1-4768-1530-5

Visit Hal Leonard Online at
**www.halleonard.com**

Contact us:
**Hal Leonard**
7777 West Bluemound Road
Milwaukee, WI 53213
Email: info@halleonard.com

In Europe, contact:
**Hal Leonard Europe Limited**
42 Wigmore Street
Marylebone, London, W1U 2RN
Email: info@halleonardeurope.com

In Australia, contact:
**Hal Leonard Australia Pty. Ltd.**
4 Lentara Court
Cheltenham, Victoria, 3192 Australia
Email: info@halleonard.com.au

# GUITAR NOTATION LEGEND

Guitar music can be notated three different ways: on a *musical staff*, in *tablature*, and in *rhythm slashes*.

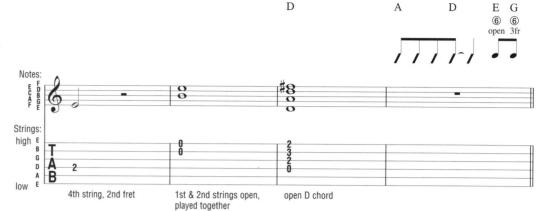

**RHYTHM SLASHES** are written above the staff. Strum chords in the rhythm indicated. Use the chord diagrams found at the top of the first page of the transcription for the appropriate chord voicings. Round noteheads indicate single notes.

**THE MUSICAL STAFF** shows pitches and rhythms and is divided by bar lines into measures. Pitches are named after the first seven letters of the alphabet.

**TABLATURE** graphically represents the guitar fingerboard. Each horizontal line represents a string, and each number represents a fret.

4th string, 2nd fret    1st & 2nd strings open, played together    open D chord

---

**HALF-STEP BEND:** Strike the note and bend up 1/2 step.

**WHOLE-STEP BEND:** Strike the note and bend up one step.

**GRACE NOTE BEND:** Strike the note and immediately bend up as indicated.

**SLIGHT (MICROTONE) BEND:** Strike the note and bend up 1/4 step.

---

**BEND AND RELEASE:** Strike the note and bend up as indicated, then release back to the original note. Only the first note is struck.

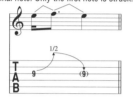

**PRE-BEND:** Bend the note as indicated, then strike it.

**VIBRATO:** The string is vibrated by rapidly bending and releasing the note with the fretting hand.

**WIDE VIBRATO:** The pitch is varied to a greater degree by vibrating with the fretting hand.

---

**HAMMER-ON:** Strike the first (lower) note with one finger, then sound the higher note (on the same string) with another finger by fretting it without picking.

**PULL-OFF:** Place both fingers on the notes to be sounded. Strike the first note and without picking, pull the finger off to sound the second (lower) note.

**LEGATO SLIDE:** Strike the first note and then slide the same fret-hand finger up or down to the second note. The second note is not struck.

**SHIFT SLIDE:** Same as legato slide, except the second note is struck.

---

**TRILL:** Very rapidly alternate between the notes indicated by continuously hammering on and pulling off.

**TAPPING:** Hammer ("tap") the fret indicated with the pick-hand index or middle finger and pull off to the note fretted by the fret hand.

**NATURAL HARMONIC:** Strike the note while the fret-hand lightly touches the string directly over the fret indicated.

**PINCH HARMONIC:** The note is fretted normally and a harmonic is produced by adding the edge of the thumb or the tip of the index finger of the pick hand to the normal pick attack.

---

**PICK SCRAPE:** The edge of the pick is rubbed down (or up) the string, producing a scratchy sound.

**MUFFLED STRINGS:** A percussive sound is produced by laying the fret hand across the string(s) without depressing, and striking them with the pick hand.

**PALM MUTING:** The note is partially muted by the pick hand lightly touching the string(s) just before the bridge.

**RAKE:** Drag the pick across the strings indicated with a single motion.

---

**TREMOLO PICKING:** The note is picked as rapidly and continuously as possible.

**VIBRATO BAR DIVE AND RETURN:** The pitch of the note or chord is dropped a specified number of steps (in rhythm), then returned to the original pitch.

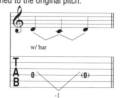

**VIBRATO BAR SCOOP:** Depress the bar just before striking the note, then quickly release the bar.

**VIBRATO BAR DIP:** Strike the note and then immediately drop a specified number of steps, then release back to the original pitch.

# STRUM AND PICK PATTERNS

This chart contains the suggested strum and pick patterns that are referred to by number at the beginning of each song in this book. The symbols ⊓ and ∨ in the strum patterns refer to down and up strokes, respectively. The letters in the pick patterns indicate which right-hand fingers play which strings.

**p** =  **thumb**
**i** = **index finger**
**m** = **middle finger**
**a** = **ring finger**

For example; Pick Pattern 2
is played: thumb - index - middle - ring

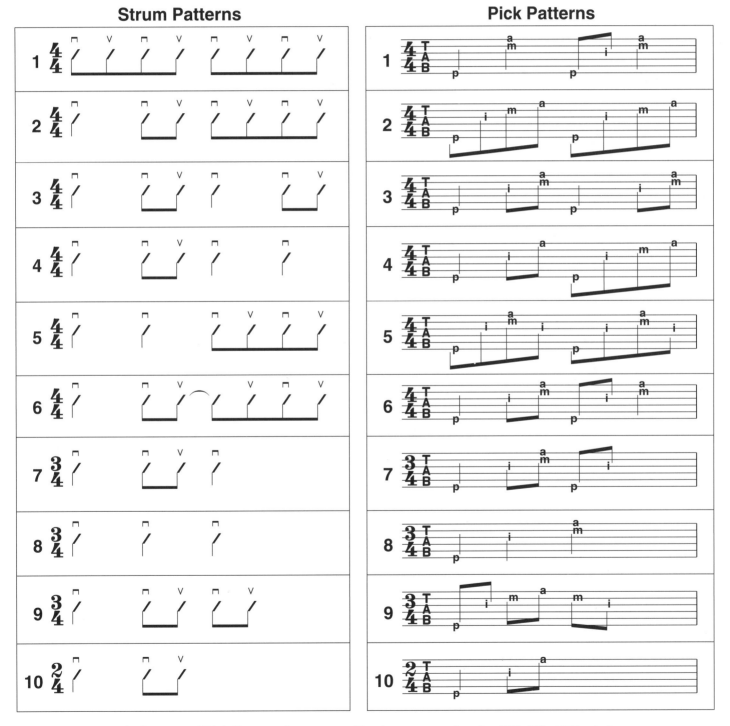

You can use the 3/4 Strum and Pick Patterns in songs written in compound meter (6/8, 9/8, 12/8, etc.).
For example, you can accompany a song in 6/8 by playing the 3/4 pattern twice in each measure.
The 4/4 Strum and Pick Patterns can be used for songs written in cut time (¢) by doubling the note
time values in the patterns. Each pattern would therefore last two measures in cut time.

# Another Brick in the Wall, Part 2

**Words and Music by Roger Waters**

**Strum Pattern: 2**
**Pick Pattern: 4**

**Chorus**
**Moderately**

We don't need __ no ed - u - ca - tion.

*Chord symbols reflect overall harmony.

We don't need __ no thought con - trol. __

No dark sar - cas - m

in the class - room.

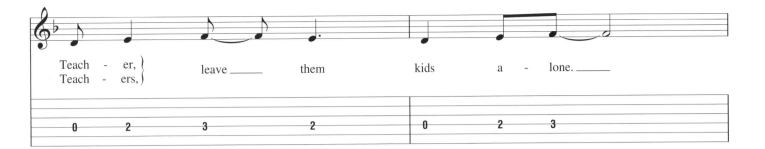

Teach - er,
Teach - ers, leave _____ them kids a - lone. _____

G

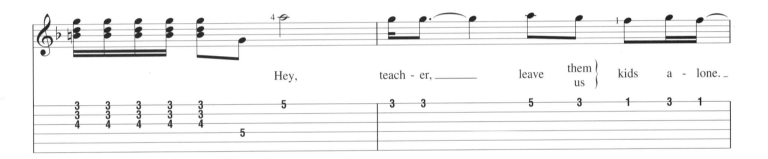

Hey, teach - er, _____ leave them us kids a - lone. _

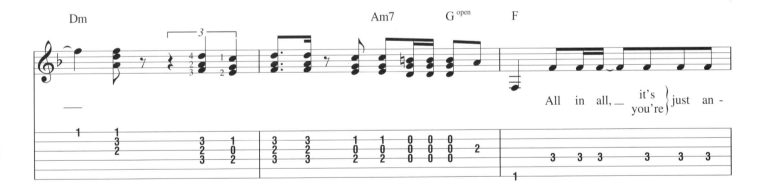

Dm                                    Am7   G^open   F

All in all, _ it's you're just an -

C                          Dm

- oth - er brick in the wall.

All in all, __ you're just an - oth - er brick in the wall.

wall.

**Guitar Solo**

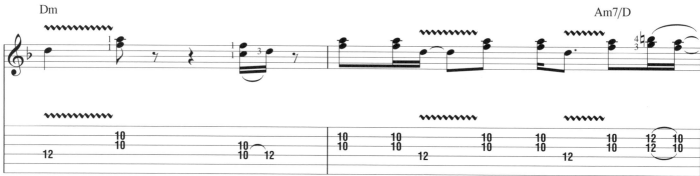

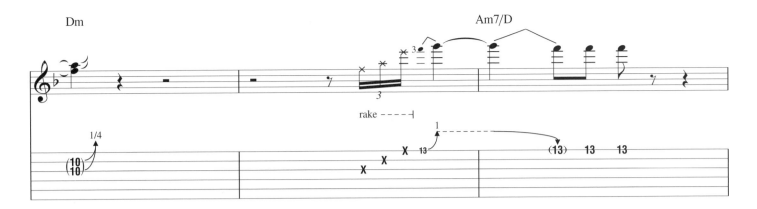

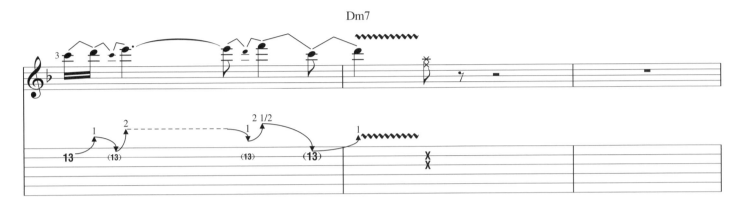

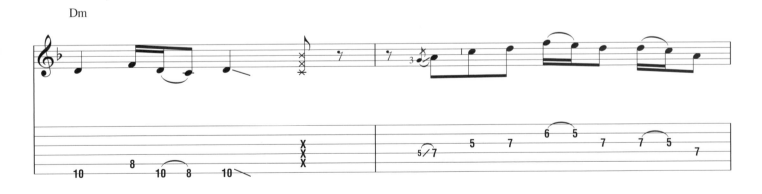

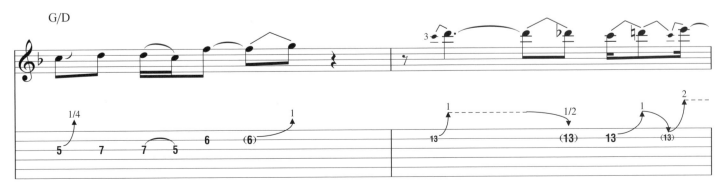

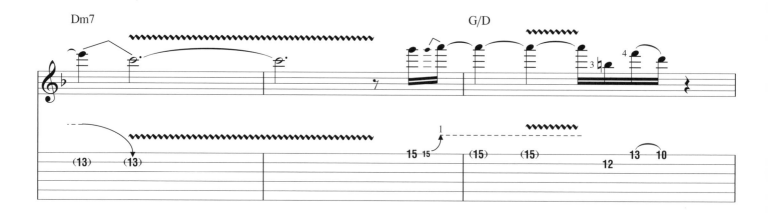

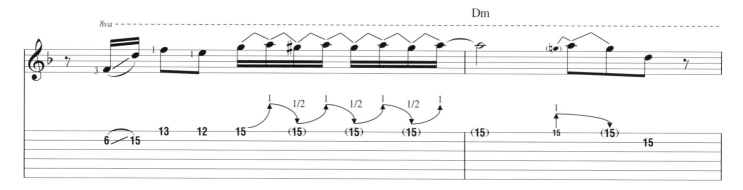

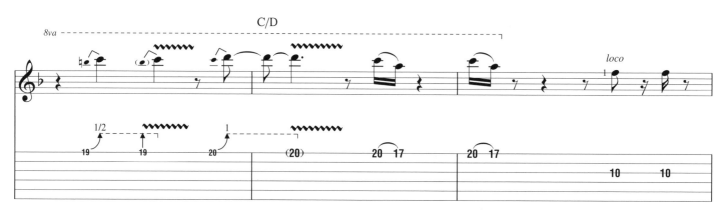

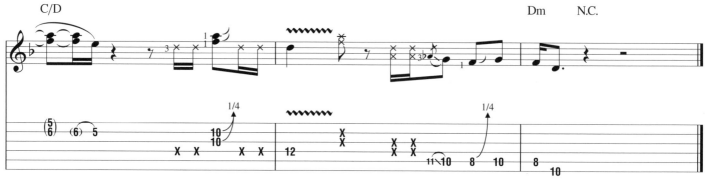

# Hey You

**Words and Music by Roger Waters**

*Capoed guitar arranged for standard tuning, next 9 meas.

1. Hey
3. Hey

**2nd time, sung one octave higher till end.

**Verse**

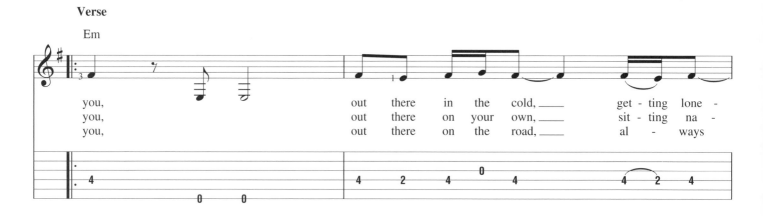

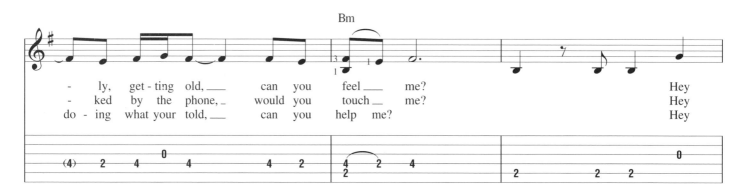

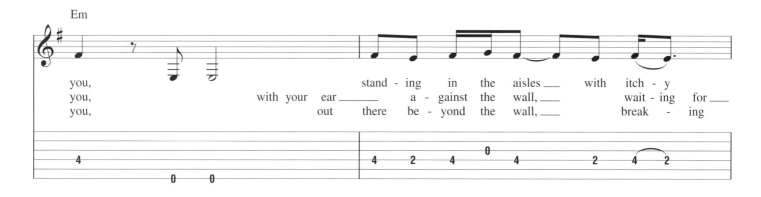

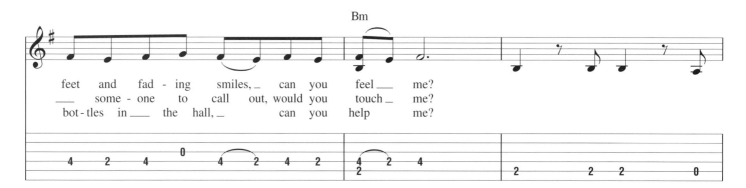

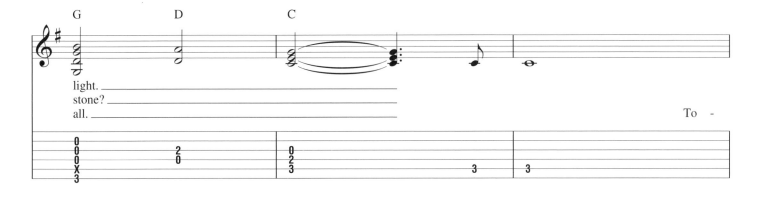

light. _____
stone? _____
all. _____ To -

*To Coda* ⊕

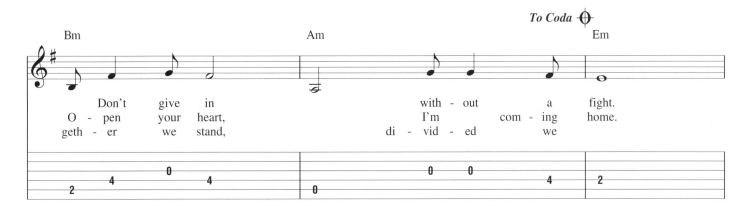

Bm                    Am                    Em

Don't    give    in                    with - out    a    fight.
O - pen    your    heart,                I'm    com - ing    home.
geth - er    we    stand,                di - vid - ed    we

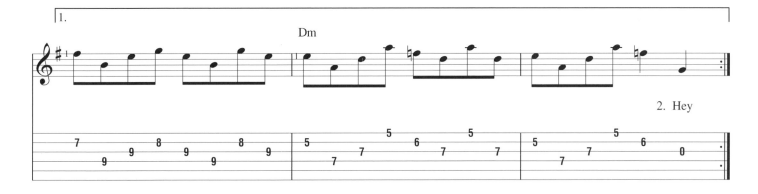

1.

Dm

2. Hey

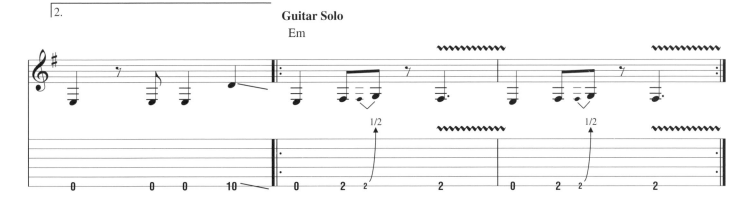

2.                    **Guitar Solo**

Em

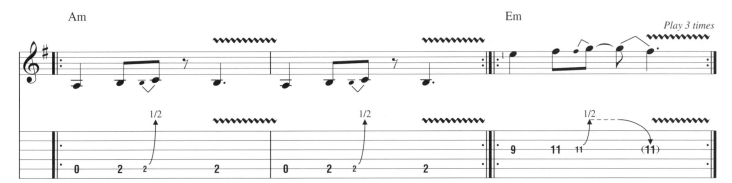

Am                                        Em        *Play 3 times*

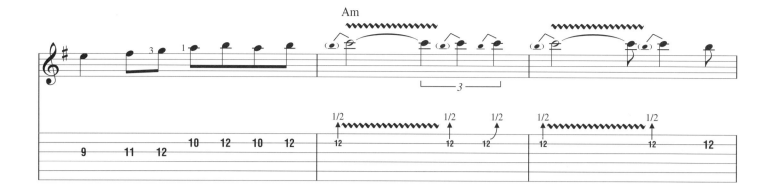

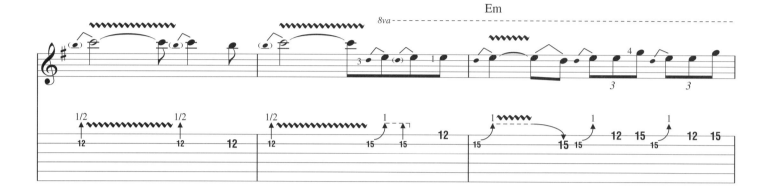

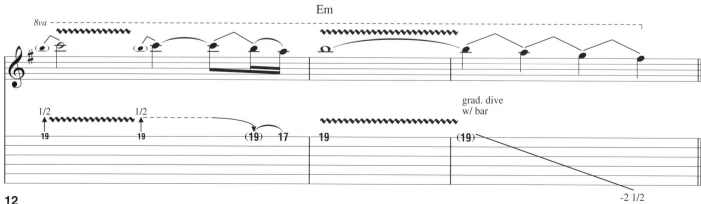

**Bridge**

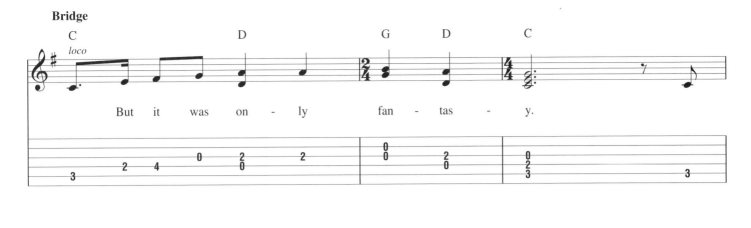

But it was on - ly fan - tas - y.

The wall was too high as you can

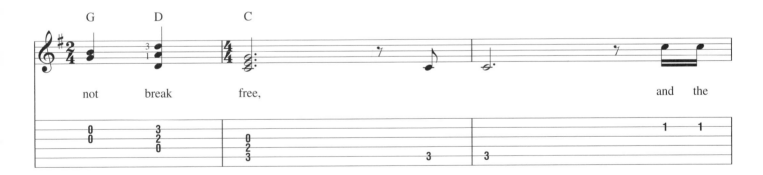

see. No mat - ter how he tried, he could

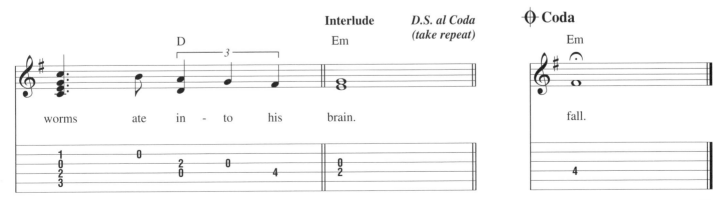

not break free, and the

**Interlude**    *D.S. al Coda* *(take repeat)*    **Coda**

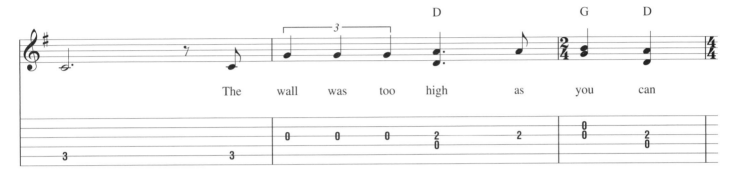

worms ate in - to his brain.      fall.

# Brain Damage

**Words and Music by Roger Waters**

**Strum Pattern: 6**
**Pick Pattern: 6**

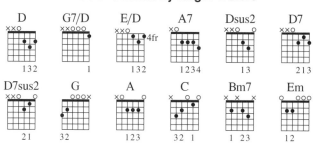

**Intro**
Slow, in 2

*Play 4 times*

1. The lu - na - tic __
2. The lu - na - tic __
3. The lu - na - tic __

__ is on the grass. __
__ is in the hall. __
__ is in my head.

The lu - na - tic _____ is on the grass. __
The lu - na - tics _____ are in my hall.
The lu - na - tic _____ is in my head.

Re - mem - ber - ing games and
The pa - per holds their fold - ed
You raise __ the blade, __

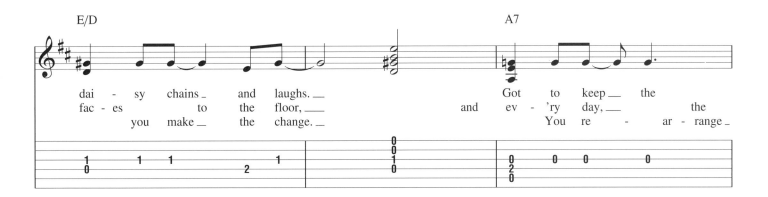

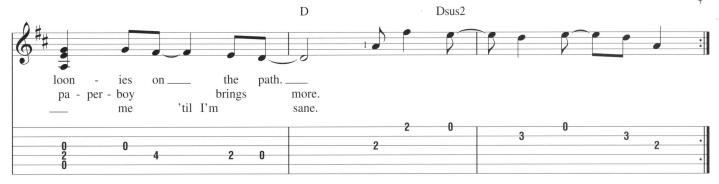

*To Coda 1*

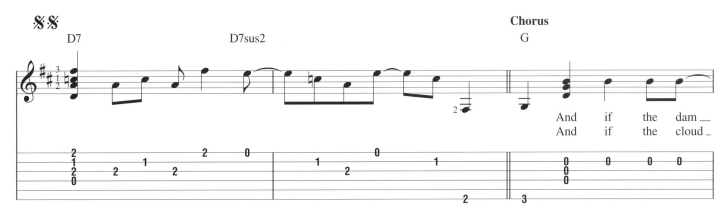

**Chorus**

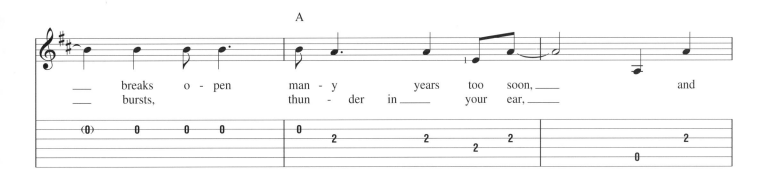

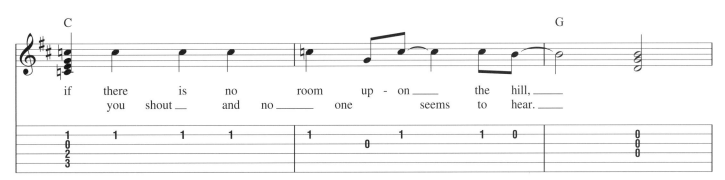

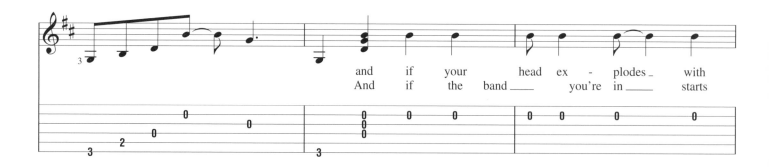

and if your head ex - plodes _ with
And if the band _ you're in _ starts

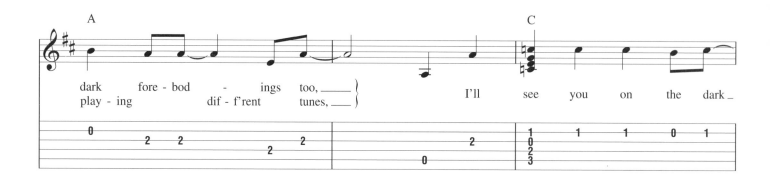

dark fore - bod - ings too, _
play - ing dif - f'rent tunes, _

I'll see you on the dark _

*To Coda 2* ⊕    *D.S. al Coda*

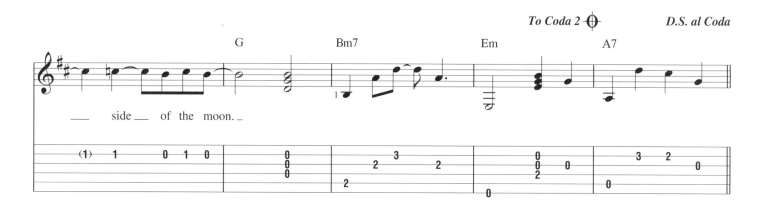

_ side _ of the moon. _

⊕ **Coda 1**

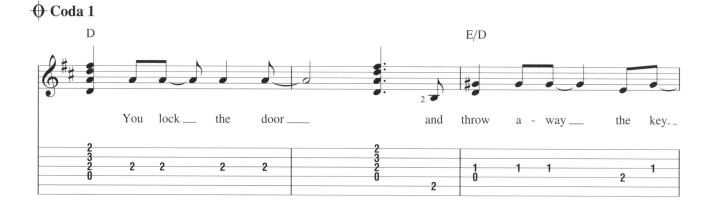

You lock _ the door _ and throw a - way _ the key.

There's some - one in my head but it's not

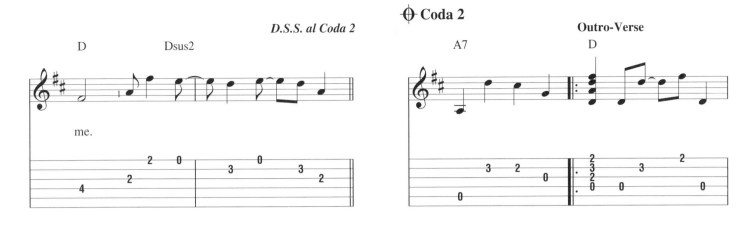

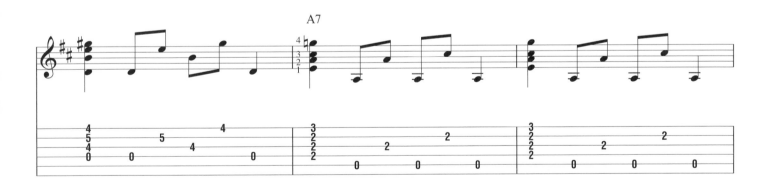

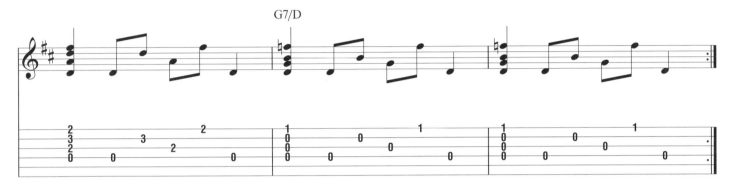

# Comfortably Numb

Words and Music by Roger Waters and David Gilmour

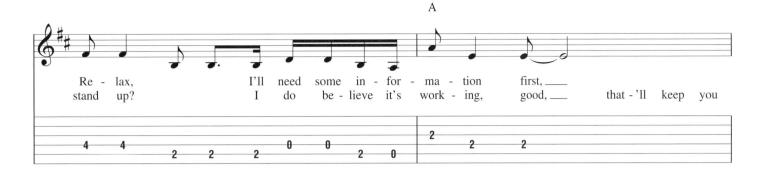

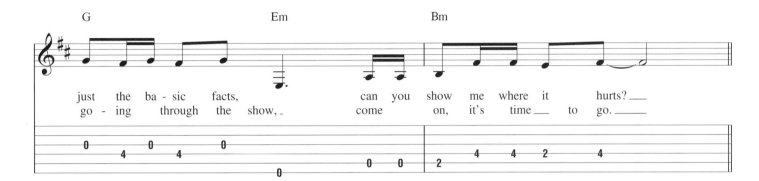

**Pre-Chorus**

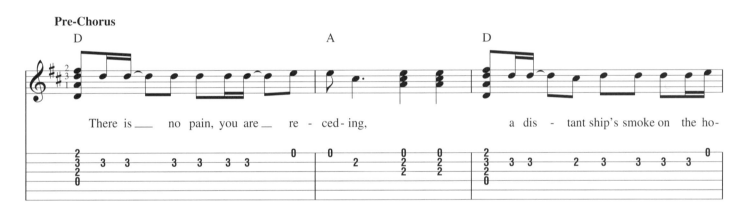

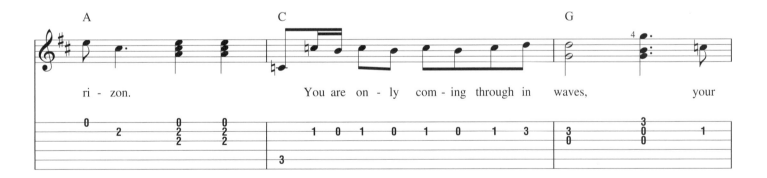

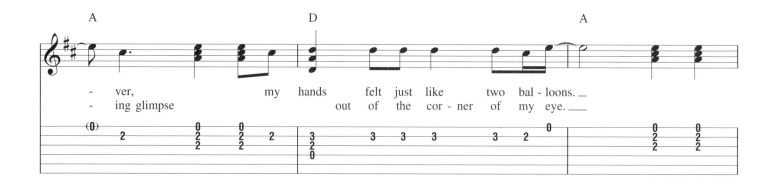

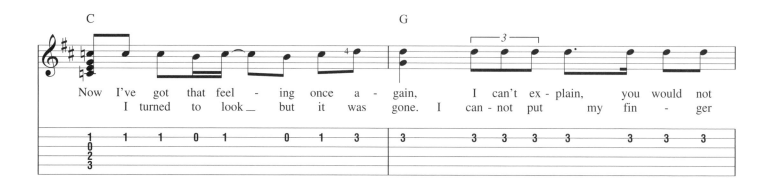

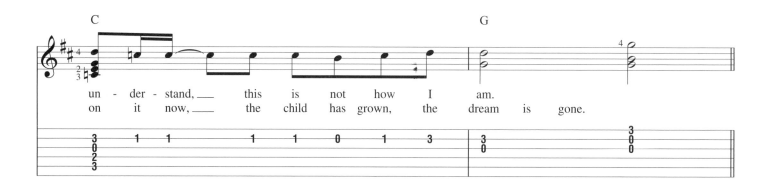

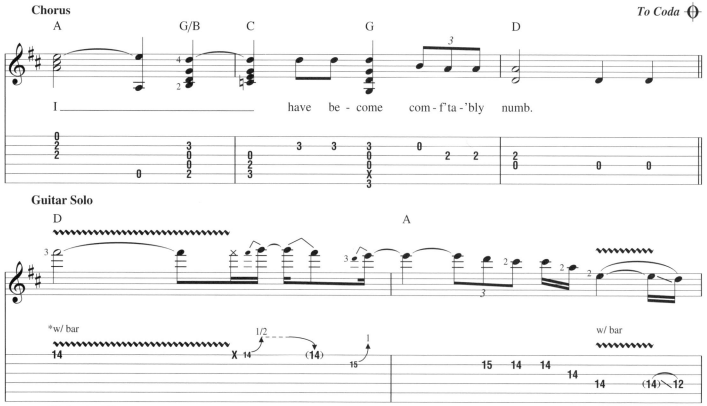

*Optional: w/ fingers

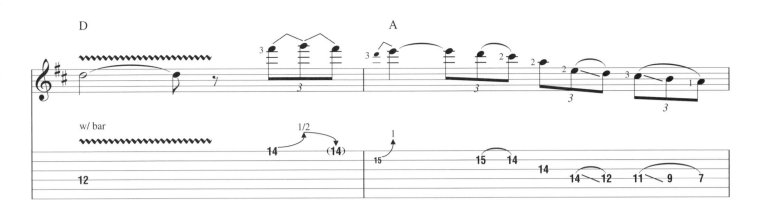

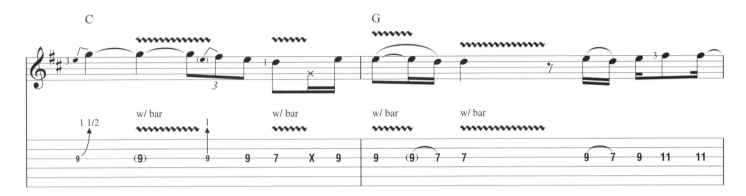

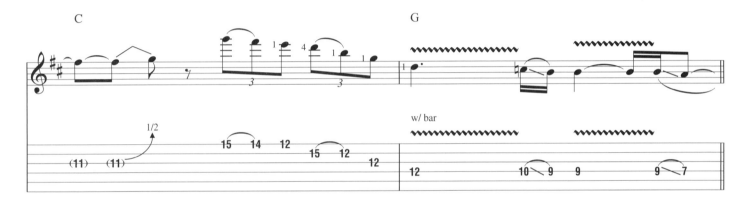

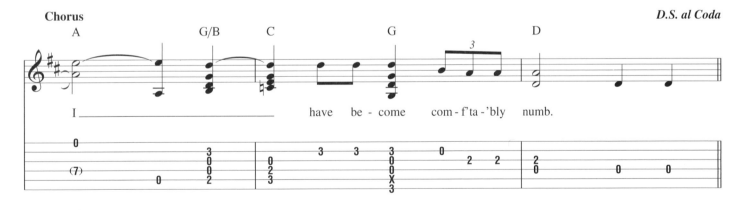

**Chorus**

*D.S. al Coda*

I _____ have be - come com - f'ta - 'bly numb.

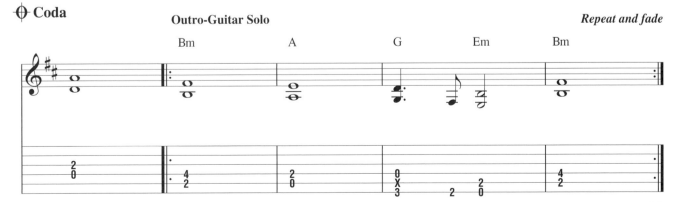

**✪ Coda**

**Outro-Guitar Solo**

*Repeat and fade*

# Have a Cigar

**Words and Music by Roger Waters**

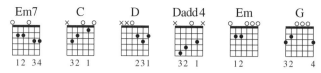

**Strum Pattern: 3**
**Pick Pattern: 3**

Intro
Moderately

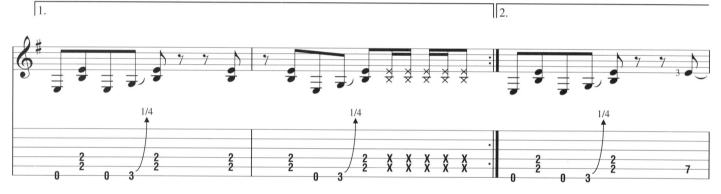

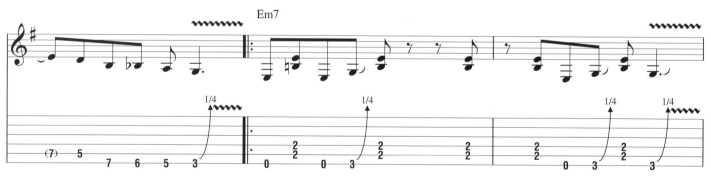

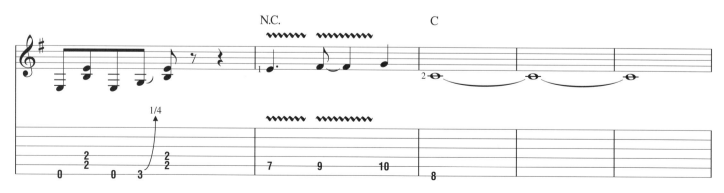

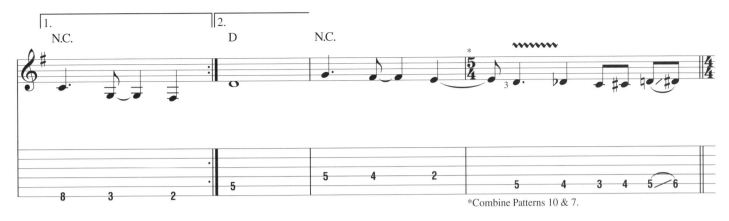

*Combine Patterns 10 & 7.

*3rd time, To Coda*

**Verse**

1. Come in here, dear boy, have a ci - gar. ___ You're gon - na
2. We're just knocked out.

go far. ___ You're gon - na fly high. ___ You're
heard a - bout the sell - out. You've got to get an al - bum out. You

nev - er gon - na die, ___ you're gon - na make it if you try. They're gon - na love you.
owe it to the peo - ple. We're so hap - py, we can hard - ly count. ___

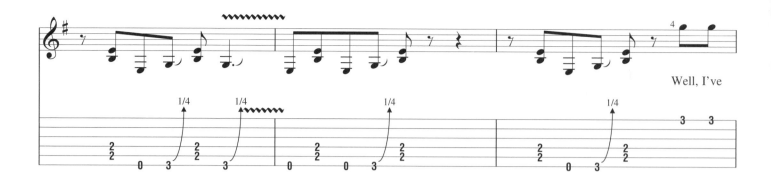

Well, I've

al - ways had a deep re-spect and I mean that most sin - cere - ly.
Ev-'ry-bod-y else is just green. _____ Have ___ you see the chart?

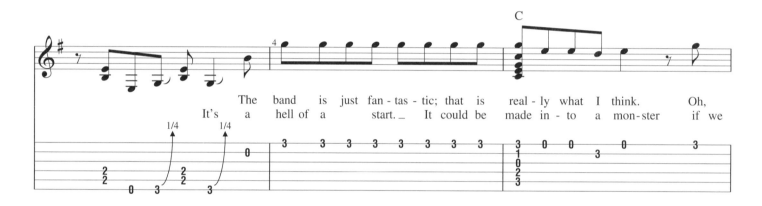

The band is just fan - tas - tic; that is real - ly what I think. Oh,
It's a hell of a start. ___ It could be made in - to a mon - ster if we

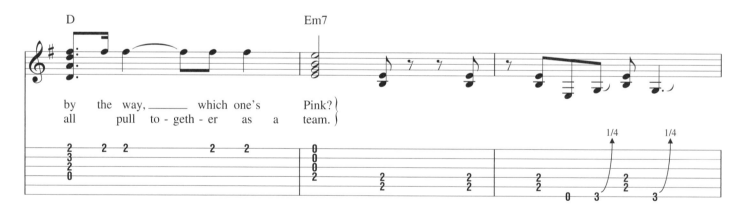

by the way, _____ which one's Pink?}
all pull to - geth - er as a team. }

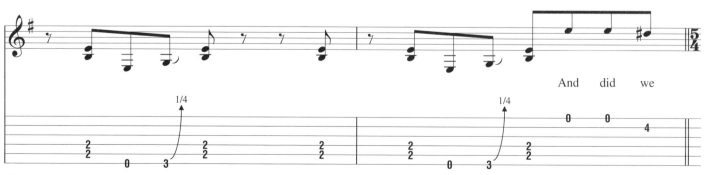

And did we

## Chorus

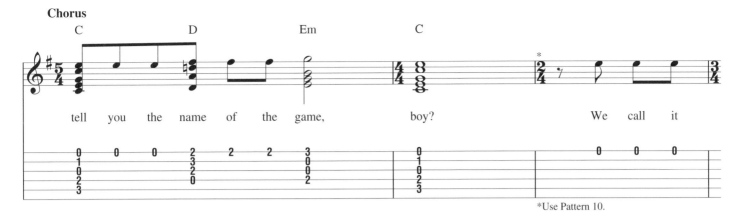

tell you the name of the game, boy? We call it

*Use Pattern 10.

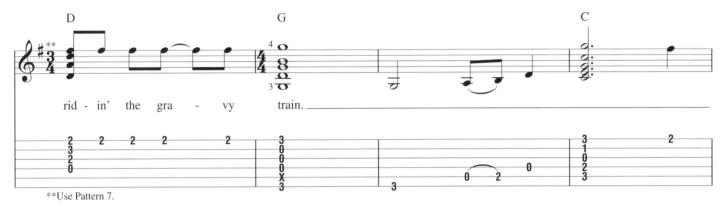

rid - in' the gra - vy train. _____

**Use Pattern 7.

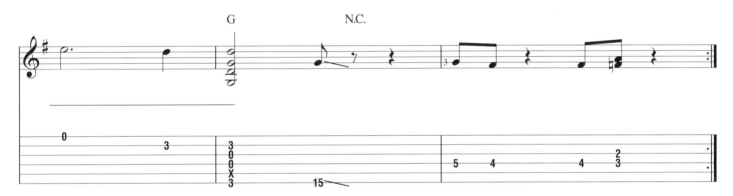

### Outro-Guitar Solo

*3rd time, D.S. al Coda
(take repeat)*

⊕ **Coda**

*D.S. and fade
(take repeat)*

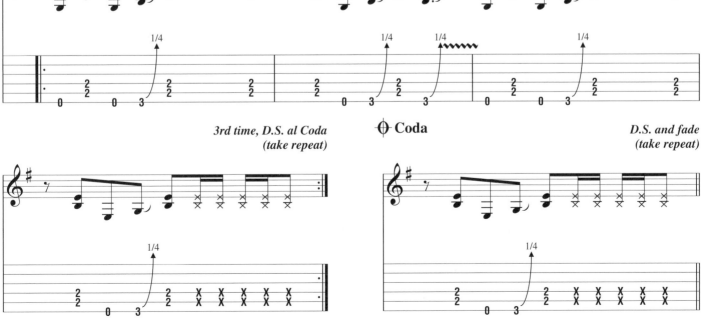

# High Hopes

**Words and Music by David Gilmour and Polly Samson**

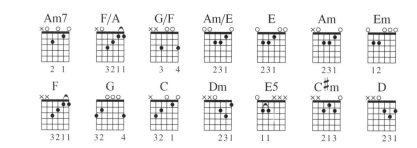

*Capo III

**Strum Pattern: 3**
**Pick Pattern: 3**

**Intro**

**Moderately slow**

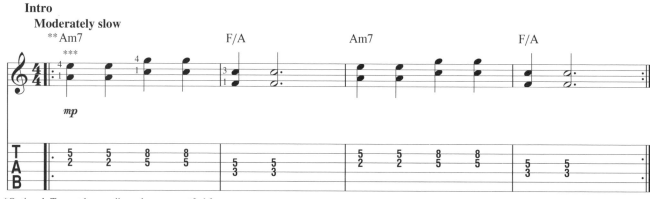

*Optional: To match recording, place capo at 3rd fret.
**Chord symbols reflect implied harmony.
***Piano arr. for gtr., next 4 meas.

**Verse**

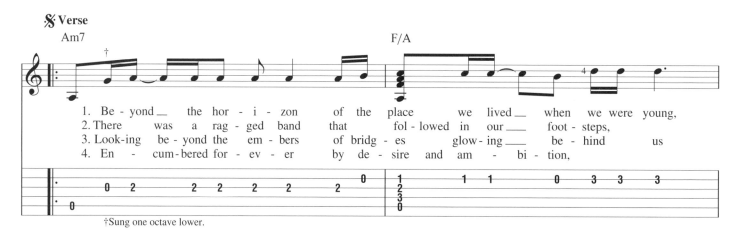

1. Be - yond ___ the hor - i - zon of the place we lived ___ when we were young,
2. There was a rag - ged band that fol - lowed in our ___ foot - steps,
3. Look - ing be - yond the em - bers of bridg - es glow - ing ___ be - hind us
4. En - cum - bered for - ev - er by de - sire and am - bi - tion,

†Sung one octave lower.

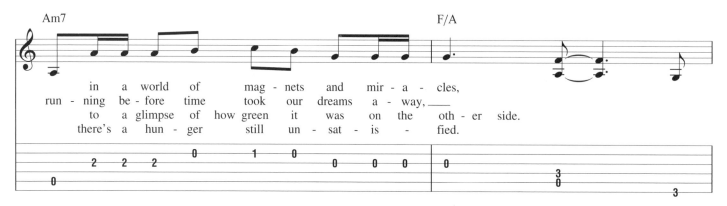

in a world of mag - nets and mir - a - cles,
run - ning be - fore time took our dreams a - way, ___
to a glimpse of how green it was on the oth - er side.
there's a hun - ger still un - sat - is - fied.

*D.C. al Coda 2*
*(no repeat)*

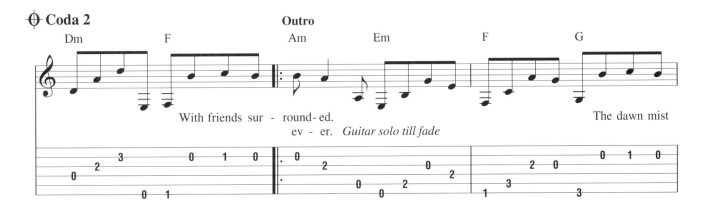

**Coda 2**                              **Outro**

With friends sur - round- ed.
ev - er. *Guitar solo till fade*                    The dawn mist

glow- ing.                                    The wa - ter flow - ing.

*Repeat and fade*

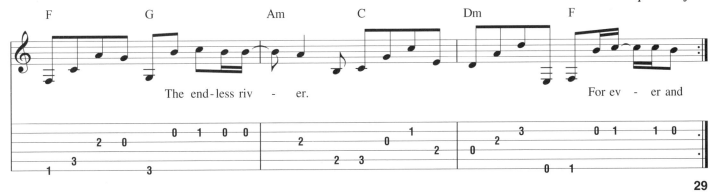

The end- less riv - er.                                    For ev - er and

# Learning to Fly

**Words and Music by David Gilmour, Anthony Moore, Bob Ezrin and Jon Carin**

*Synth arr. for gtr., next 2 meas.

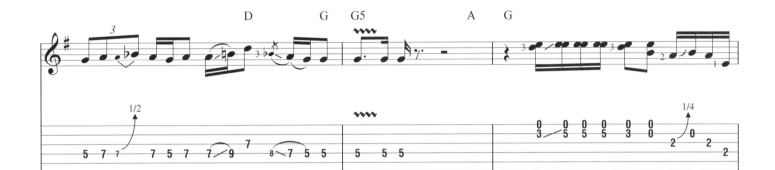

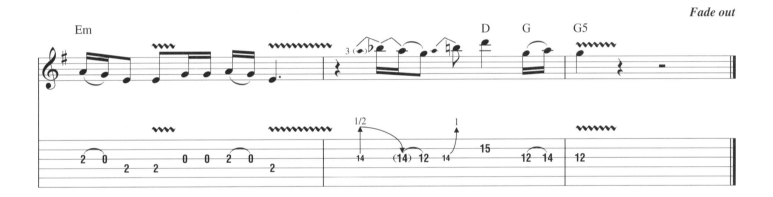

*Additional Lyrics*

2. Ice is forming on the tips of my wings.
Unheeded warnings, I thought I thought of ev'rything.
No navigator to find my way home.
Unladened, empty and turned to stone.

*Chorus 2*  A soul in tension that's learning to fly.
Condition grounded but determined to try.
Can't keep my eyes from the circling skies.
Tongue-tied and twisted, just an Earth-bound misfit, I.

3. Above the planet on a wing and a prayer.
My grubby halo, a vapor trail in the empty air.
Across the clouds, I see my shadow fly
Out of the corner of my watering eye.
I dream unthreatened by the morning light.
Could blow this soul right through the roof of the night.

*Chorus 3*  There's no sensation to compare with this.
Suspend animation, a state of bliss.
Can't keep my mind from the circling skies.
Tongue-tied and twisted, just an Earth-bound misfit, I.

# Money

**Words and Music by Roger Waters**

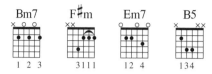

**\*Strum Pattern: 4 & 8**
**\*Pick Pattern: 3 & 8**

*Combine patterns for 7/4 meas.

\*\*Bass arr. for gtr., next 2 meas.

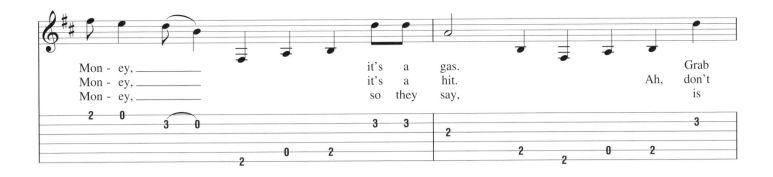

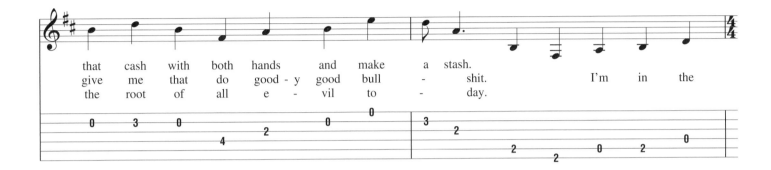

**To Coda** ⊕

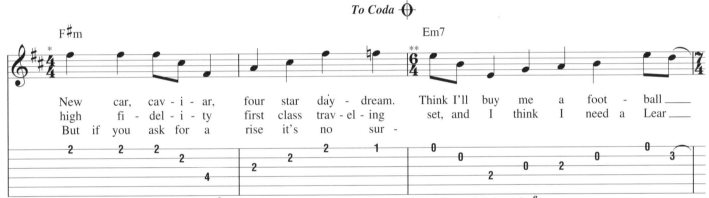

*Use Strum Pattern 4, Pick Pattern 3 for 4/4 meas.   **Play Pattern 8 (2 times) for 6/4 meas.

**Saxophone Solo**

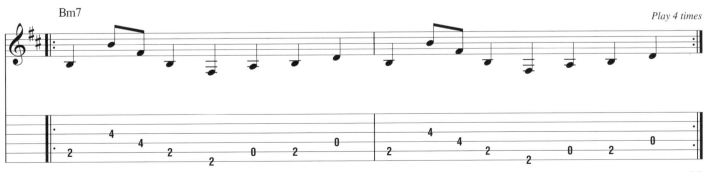

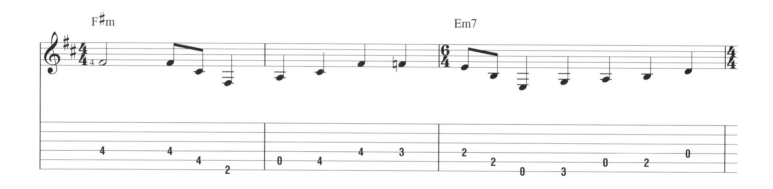

**Guitar Solo**

2nd & 3rd times, ad lib.

Bm7

w/ reverb & delay

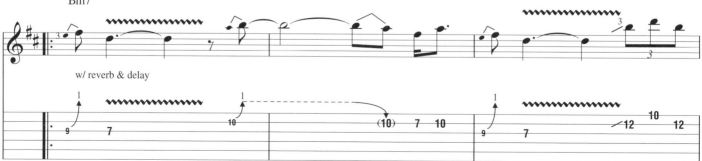

36

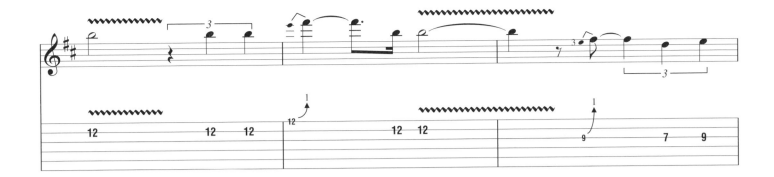

Em7

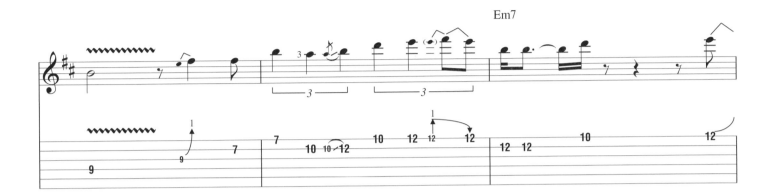

Bm7

F#m

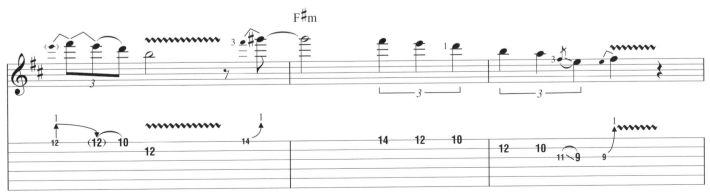

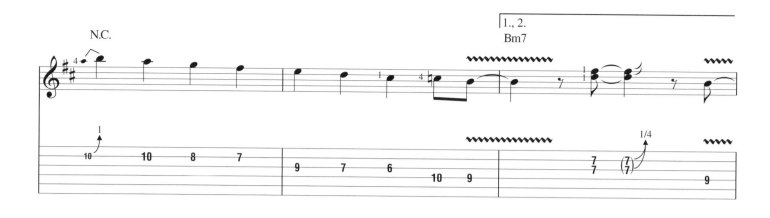

prise that they're giv - ing none a - way, _ a - way, _ a -

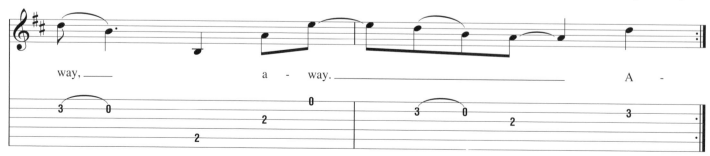

way, _ a - way. _ A -

# Us and Them

**Words by Roger Waters**
**Music by Roger Waters and Rick Wright**

**Strum Pattern: 5**
**Pick Pattern: 5**

*Intro
Slow

*let ring throughout*

*2nd time, **Sax Solo**.

**Verse**
Dsus2

1. Us                                            and
3. Black                                         and
5. *Piano solo*
7. *See additional lyrics*

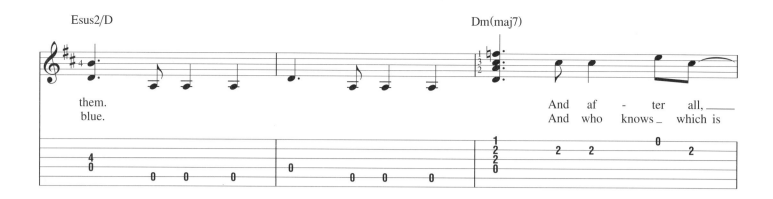

them.
blue.

And af - ter all,
And who knows which is

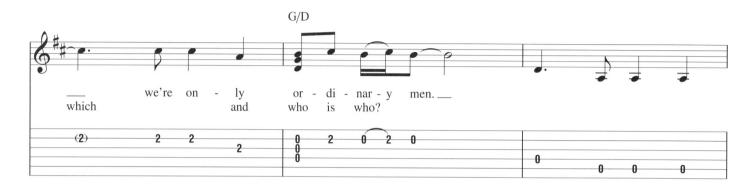

which we're on - ly or - di - nar - y men.
which and who is who?

**Verse**
Dsus2

2. Me
4. Up
6. *Sax solo*
8. *See additional lyrics*

and you.
and down.

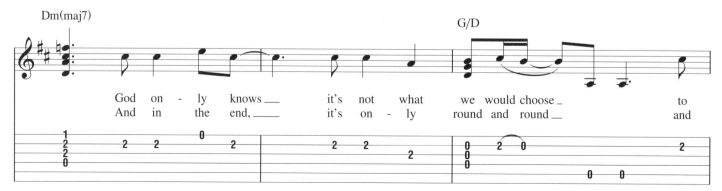

God on - ly knows it's not what we would choose to
And in the end, it's on - ly round and round and

**Bridge**

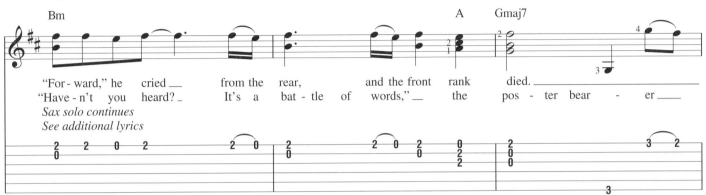

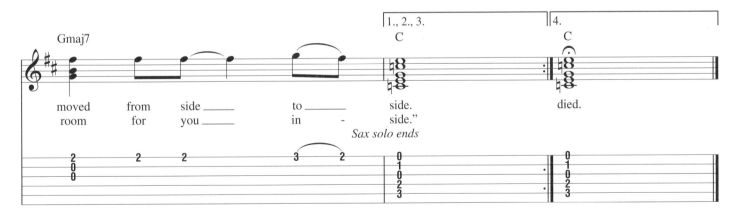

*Additional Lyrics*

7. Down and out.
   It can't be helped,
   But there's a lot of it about.

8. With, without.
   And who'll deny
   It's what the fighting's all about.

*Bridge* Out of the way, it's a busy day.
   I've got things on my mind.
   For want of the price of tea and a slice,
   The old man died.

# Mother

**Words and Music by Roger Waters**

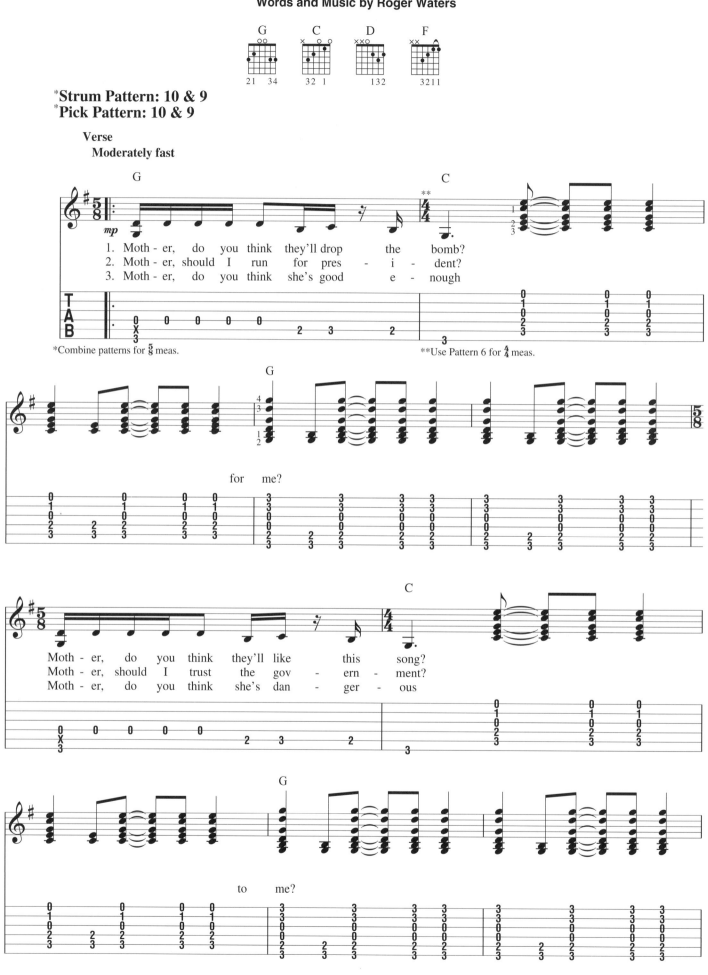

*Strum Pattern: 10 & 9
*Pick Pattern: 10 & 9

Verse
Moderately fast

1. Moth - er, do you think they'll drop the bomb?
2. Moth - er, should I run for pres - i - dent?
3. Moth - er, do you think she's good e - nough

*Combine patterns for ⅝ meas.

**Use Pattern 6 for 4/4 meas.

for me?

Moth - er, do you think they'll like this song?
Moth - er, should I trust the gov - ern - ment?
Moth - er, do you think she's dan - ger - ous

to me?

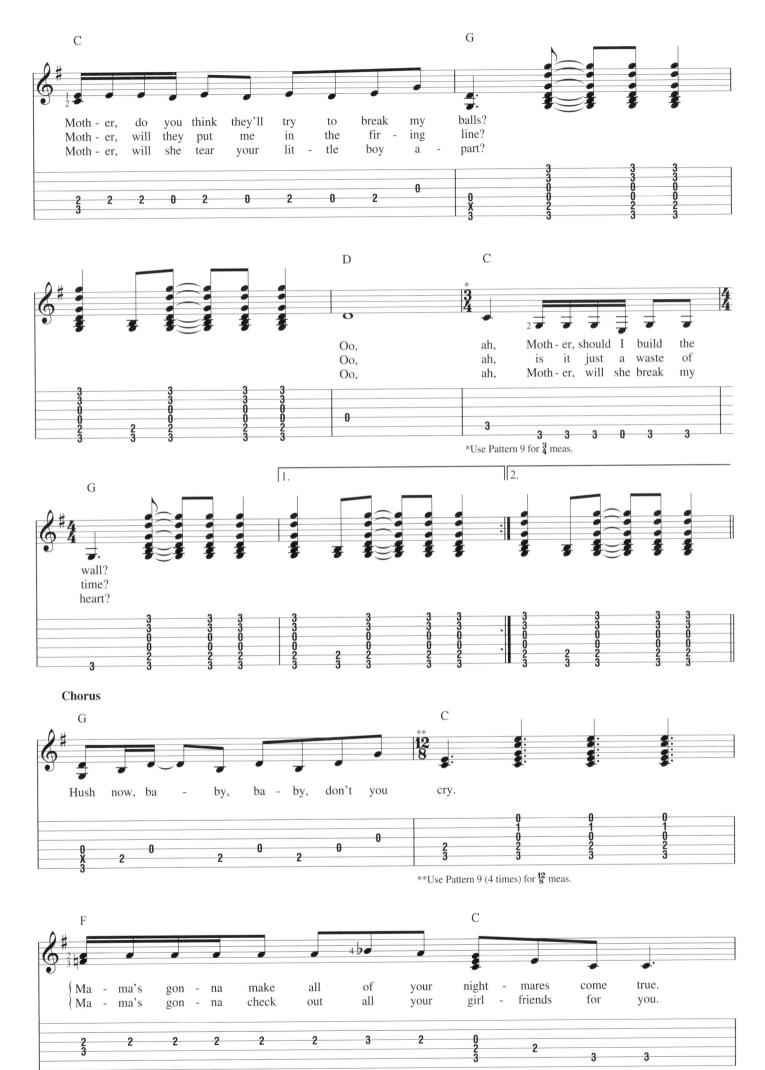

Ma - ma's gon - na put all of her fears in - to you.
Ma - ma won't let an - y - one dir - ty get through.

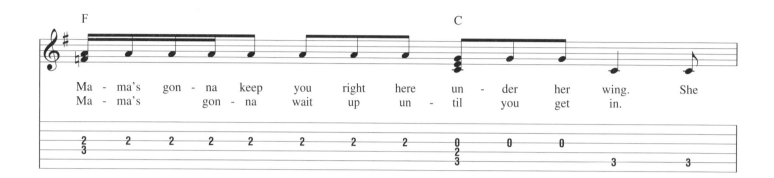

Ma - ma's gon - na keep you right here un - der her wing. She
Ma - ma's gon - na wait up un - til you get in.

won't let you fly, but she might let you sing.
Ma - ma will al - ways find out let where you've been.

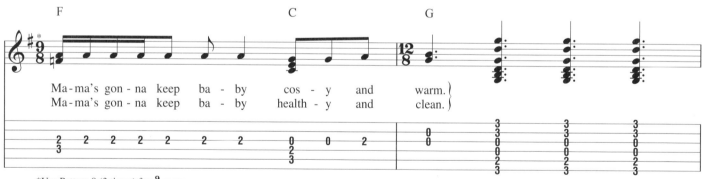

Ma - ma's gon - na keep ba - by cos - y and warm.}
Ma - ma gon - na keep ba - by health - y and clean.}

*Use Pattern 9 (3 times) for $\frac{9}{8}$ meas.

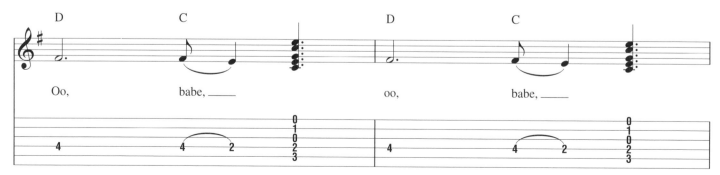

Oo, babe, _____ oo, babe, _____

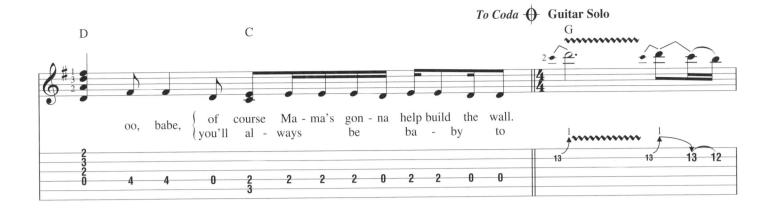

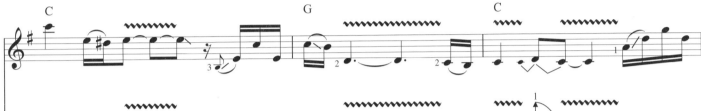

oo, babe, { of course Ma - ma's gon - na help build the wall.
{ you'll al - ways be ba - by to

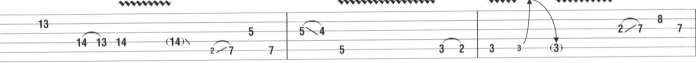

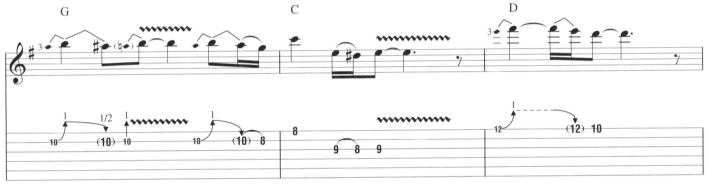

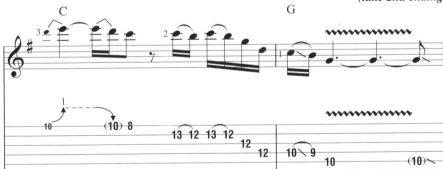

me.

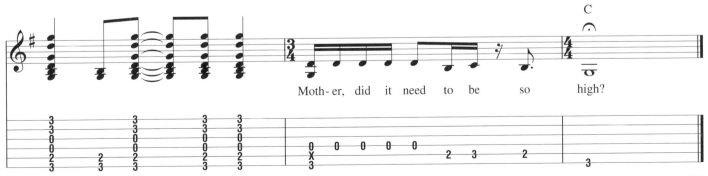

Moth - er, did it need to be so high?

# Run Like Hell

### Words and Music by Roger Waters and David Gilmour

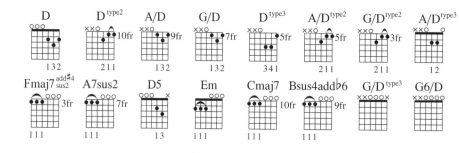

Drop D tuning:
(low to high) D-A-D-G-B-E

**Strum Pattern: 5**
**Pick Pattern: 1**

Intro
Moderately

*Pick note on repeat.

4th time, To Coda 2

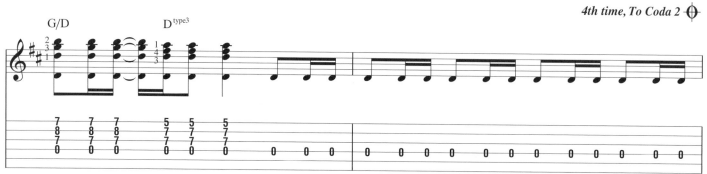

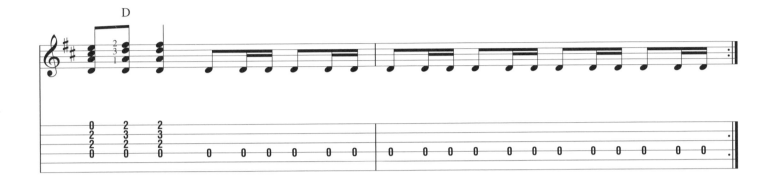

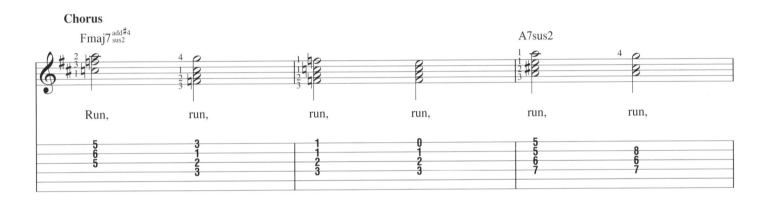

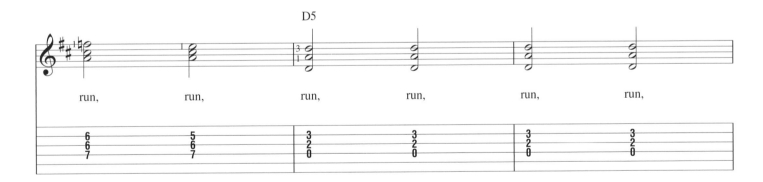

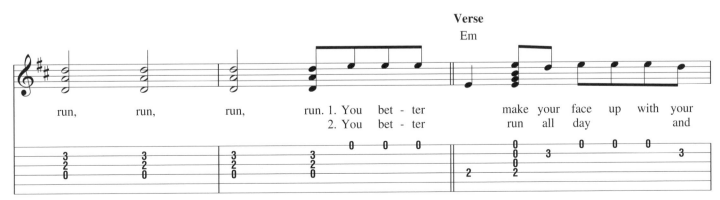

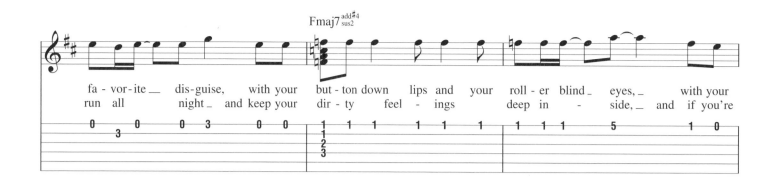

fa - vor - ite ___ dis - guise, with your but - ton down lips and your roll - er blind eyes, ___ with your
run all night ___ and keep your dir - ty feel - ings deep in - side, ___ and if you're

emp - ty smile ___ and your hun - gry heart. ___ Feel the bi - le ris - ing from your
tak - ing your girl - friend out to - night ___ you'd bet - ter park the car ___ well

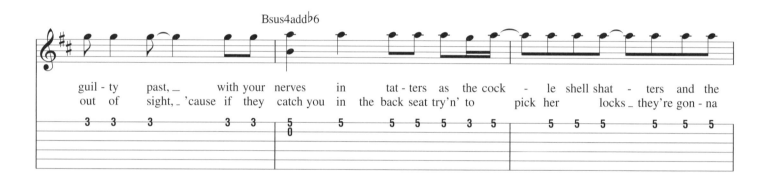

guil - ty past, ___ with your nerves in tat - ters as the cock - le shell shat - ters and the
out of sight, ___ 'cause if they catch you in the back seat try'n' to pick her locks ___ they're gon - na

**Interlude**

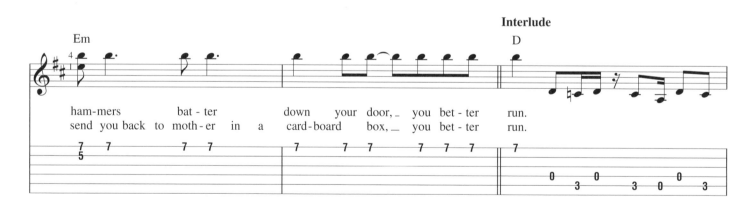

ham - mers bat - ter down your door, ___ you bet - ter run.
send you back to moth - er in a card - board box, ___ you bet - ter run.

*To Coda 1* &#x2295;          *D.S. al Coda 1*
(*no repeat*)

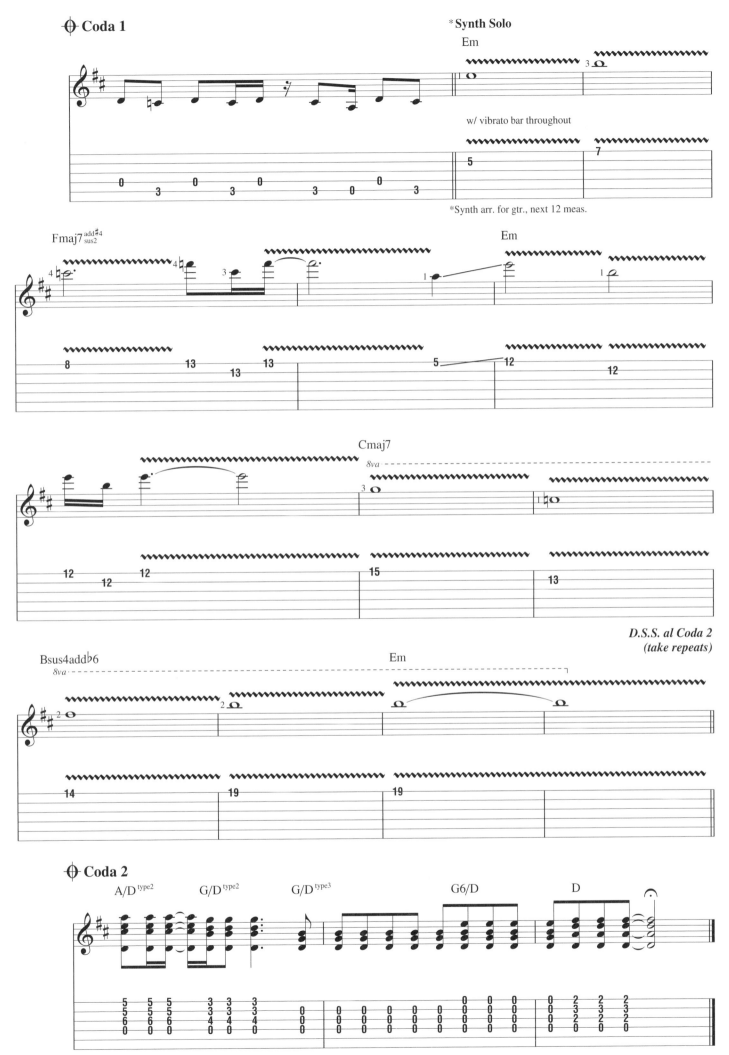

# Time

**Words and Music by Roger Waters, Nicholas Mason, David Gilmour and Rick Wright**

**𝄋 Verse**

1. Tick - ing a - way ___ the mo - ments that make up a dull day. (You)
run, you run ___ to catch up with the sun, but it's sink - ing. (And)

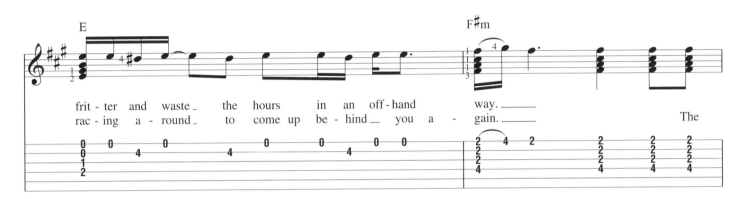

frit - ter and waste ___ the hours in an off - hand way. ___
rac - ing a - round ___ to come up be - hind ___ you a - gain. ___ The

Kick - ing a - round ___ on a piece of ground in your home - town,
sun is the same ___ in a rel - a - tive way, but you're old - er,

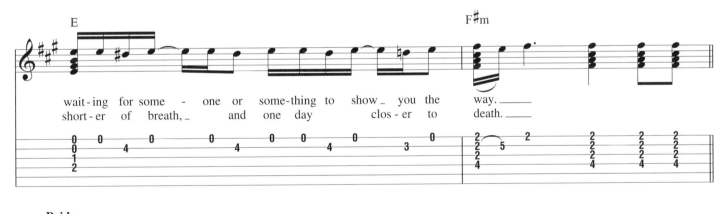

wait - ing for some - one or some - thing to show ___ you the way. ___
short - er of breath, ___ and one day clos - er to death. ___

**Bridge**

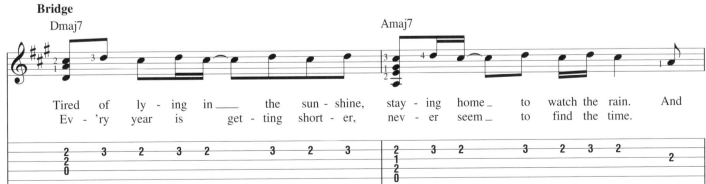

Tired of ly - ing in ___ the sun - shine, stay - ing home ___ to watch the rain. And
Ev - 'ry year is get - ting short - er, nev - er seem ___ to find the time.

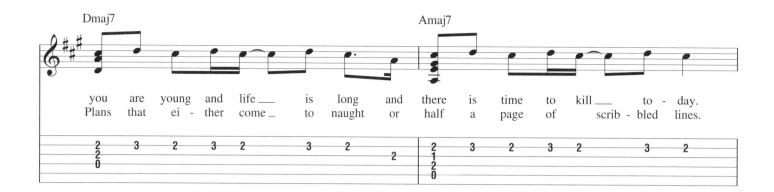

you are young and life __ is long and there is time to kill __ to - day.
Plans that ei - ther come __ to naught or half a page of scrib - bled lines.

And then one day you find __ ten years have got __ be - hind you.
Hang - ing on in qui - et des - par - a - tion is the Eng - lish way. The

*To Coda*

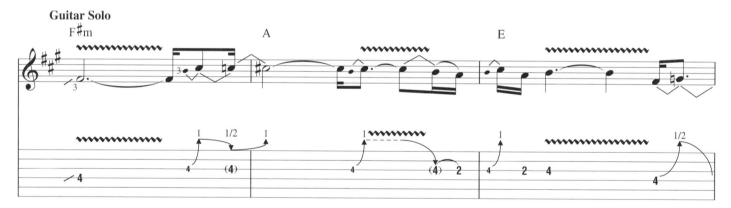

No one told you when __ to run. You missed the start - ing gun.
time is gone, the song is o - ver.

**Guitar Solo**

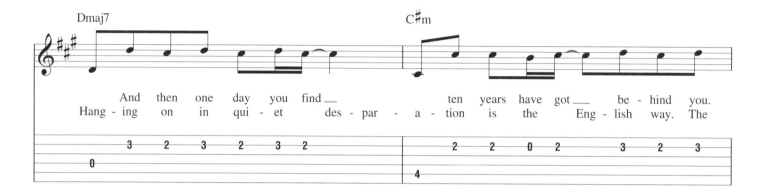

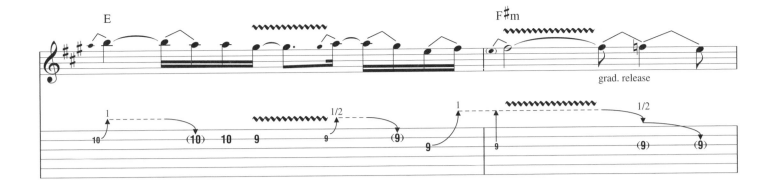

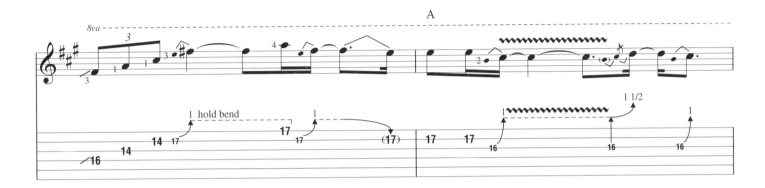

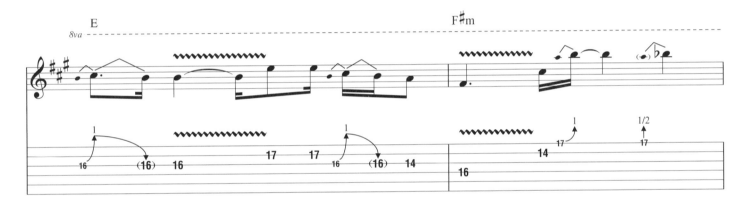

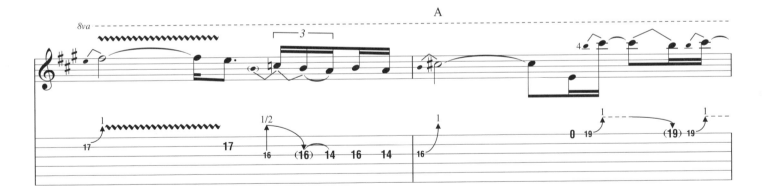

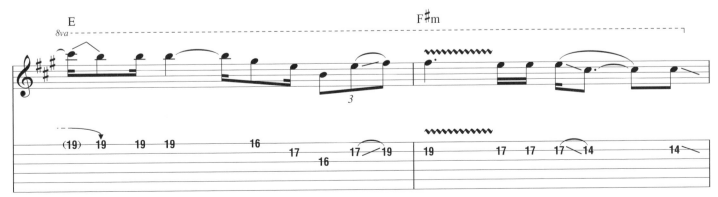

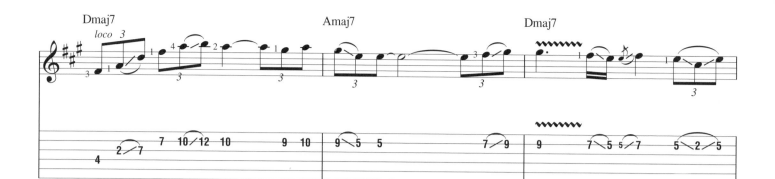

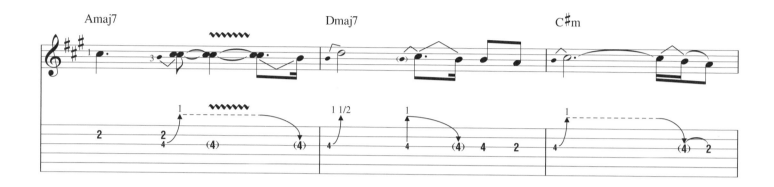

D.S. al Coda

2. And you

Coda

Breathe (Reprise)
A tempo
*Em        A7

Thought I'd some-thing more to say. _

*Chord symbols reflect basic harmony.

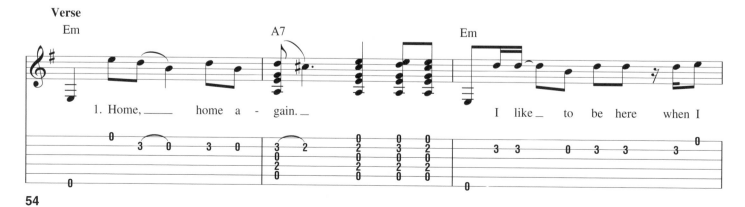

Verse
Em        A7        Em

1. Home, _____ home a - gain. _        I like _ to be here when I

can. _____ And when _____ I come home cold and

tired, _____ it's good to warm _____ my bones be - side _____ the

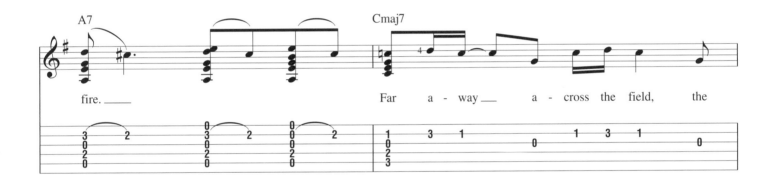

fire. _____ Far a - way _____ a - cross the field, the

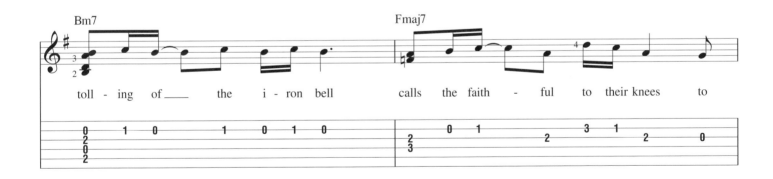

toll - ing of _____ the i - ron bell calls the faith - ful to their knees to

hear the soft - ly spok - en mag - ic spell.

# Young Lust

### Words and Music by Roger Waters and David Gilmour

**Strum Pattern: 5**
**Pick Pattern: 1**

## Coda 1

**Guitar Solo**

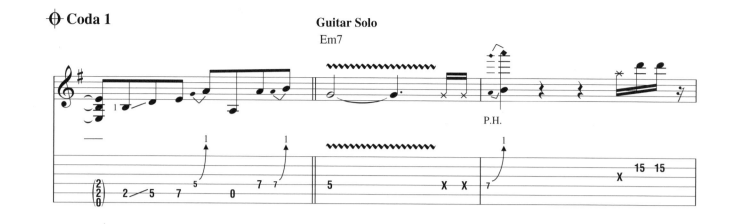

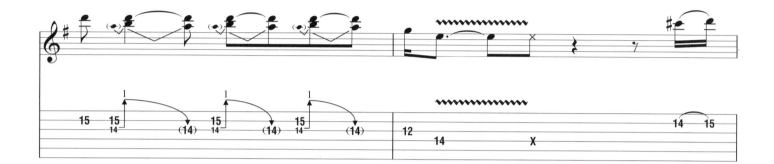

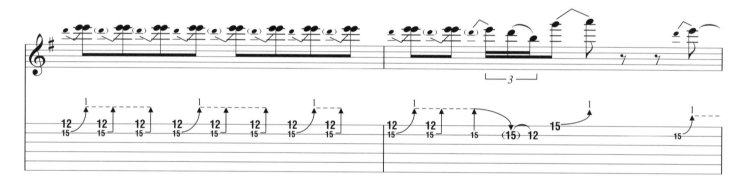

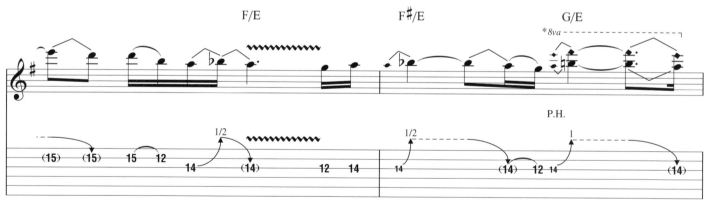

*Applies to top notes only.

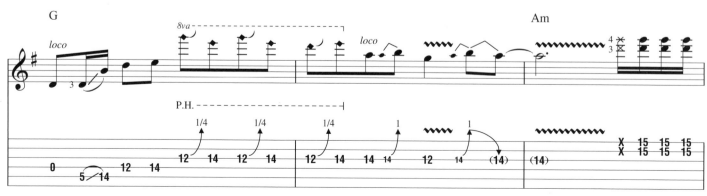

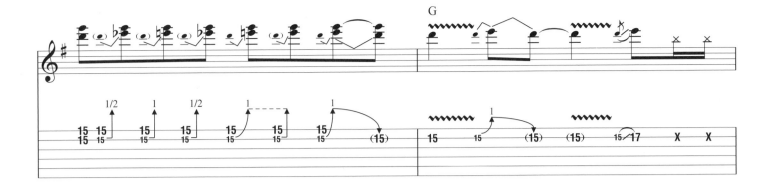

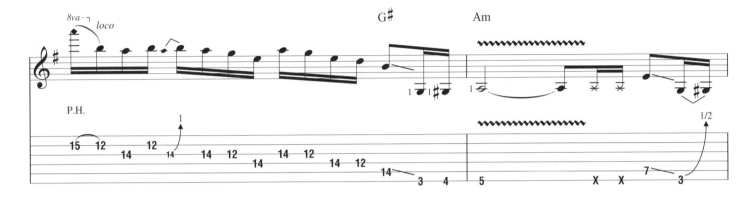

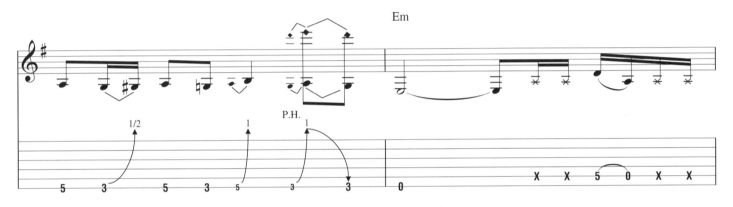

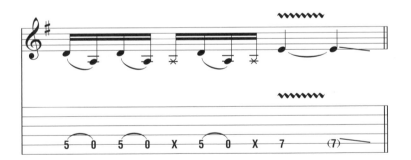

**D.S.S. al Coda 2**

### ⊕ Coda 2

**Outro**
w/ ad lib. on repeats

N.C.(E5)

*Repeat and fade*

# Wish You Were Here

**Words and Music by Roger Waters and David Gilmour**

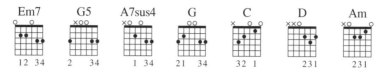

**Strum Pattern: 1**
**Pick Pattern: 5**

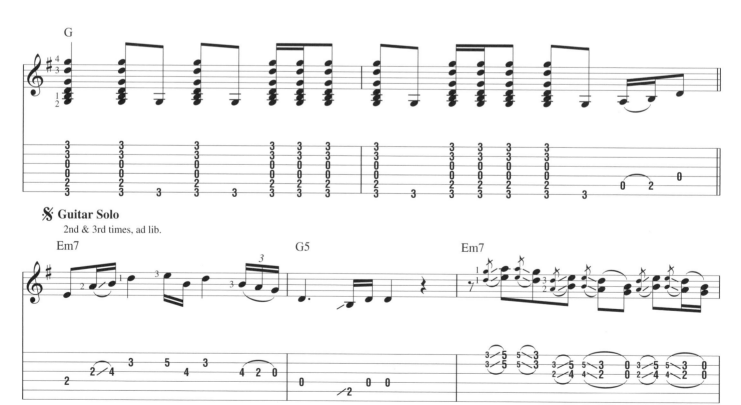

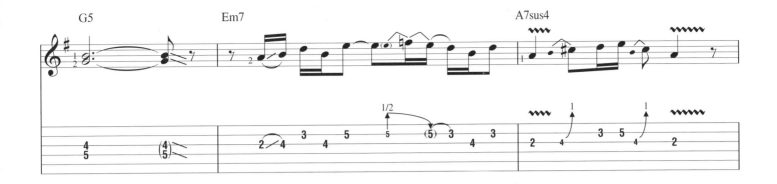

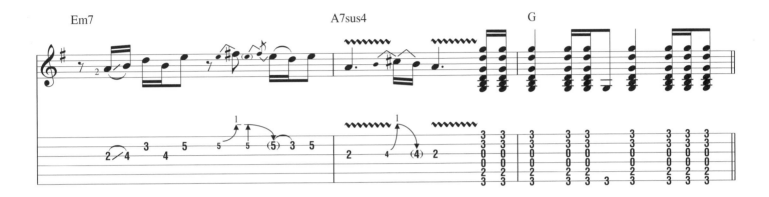

**Verse**

1. So, _____ so you think you can tell _____ heav - en from
3. How I wish, how I wish you were here. _____ We're just

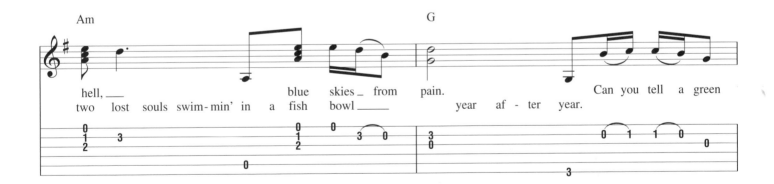

hell, ___ blue skies _ from pain. Can you tell a green
two lost souls swim-min' in a fish bowl _____ year af - ter year.

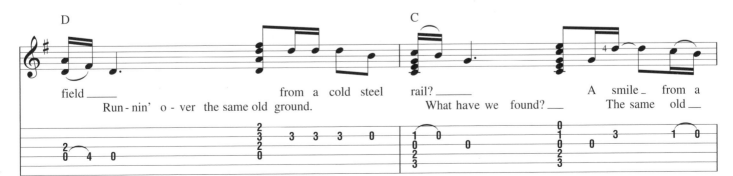

field _____ from a cold steel rail? _____ A smile _ from a
Run - nin' o - ver the same old ground. What have we found? ___ The same old __

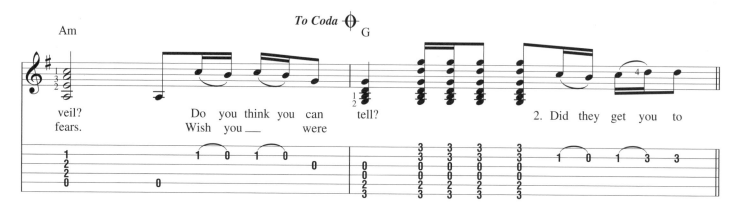

*To Coda* ⊕ G

veil? ......... Do you think you can tell?
fears. ......... Wish you ___ were

2. Did they get you to

**Verse**

C                 D                 Am

trade ___ your he - roes for ghosts? ___ Hot ash-es for trees? ___ Hot air for a

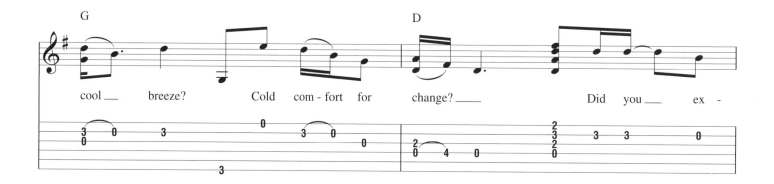

G                      D

cool ___ breeze? Cold com - fort for change? ___ Did you ___ ex -

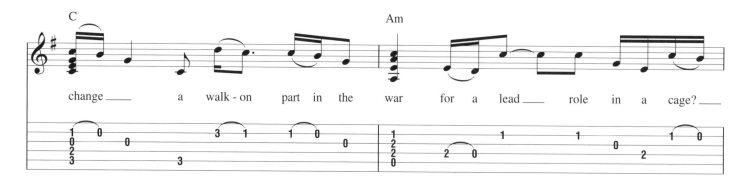

C                      Am

change ___ a walk - on part in the war for a lead ___ role in a cage? ___

*D.S. al Coda*              ⊕ **Coda**                 *D.S.S. and fade on Guitar Solo*
                                                                   *(take repeat)*

G                                                    G

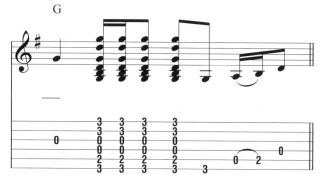

___                                                           here. ___

## EASY GUITAR WITH NOTES & TAB

*This series features simplified arrangements with notes, tab, chord charts, and strum and pick patterns.*

## MIXED FOLIOS

| | | |
|---|---|---|
| 00702287 Acoustic | $16.99 |
| 00702002 Acoustic Rock Hits for Easy Guitar | $15.99 |
| 00702166 All-Time Best Guitar Collection | $19.99 |
| 00702232 Best Acoustic Songs for Easy Guitar | $14.99 |
| 00119835 Best Children's Songs | $16.99 |
| 00702233 Best Hard Rock Songs | $15.99 |
| 00703055 The Big Book of Nursery Rhymes & Children's Songs | $16.99 |
| 00698978 Big Christmas Collection | $17.99 |
| 00702394 Bluegrass Songs for Easy Guitar | $12.99 |
| 00289632 Bohemian Rhapsody | $17.99 |
| 00703387 Celtic Classics | $14.99 |
| 00224808 Chart Hits of 2016-2017 | $14.99 |
| 00267383 Chart Hits of 2017-2018 | $14.99 |
| 00334293 Chart Hits of 2019-2020 | $16.99 |
| 00702149 Children's Christian Songbook | $9.99 |
| 00702028 Christmas Classics | $8.99 |
| 00101779 Christmas Guitar | $14.99 |
| 00702185 Christmas Hits | $10.99 |
| 00702141 Classic Rock | $8.95 |
| 00159642 Classical Melodies | $12.99 |
| 00253933 Disney/Pixar's Coco | $16.99 |
| 00702203 CMT's 100 Greatest Country Songs | $29.99 |
| 00702283 The Contemporary Christian Collection | $16.99 |
| 00196954 Contemporary Disney | $19.99 |

| | | |
|---|---|---|
| 00702239 Country Classics for Easy Guitar | $22.99 |
| 00702257 Easy Acoustic Guitar Songs | $14.99 |
| 00702280 Easy Guitar Tab White Pages | $29.99 |
| 00702041 Favorite Hymns for Easy Guitar | $10.99 |
| 00222701 Folk Pop Songs | $14.99 |
| 00126894 Frozen | $14.99 |
| 00333922 Frozen 2 | $14.99 |
| 00702286 Glee | $16.99 |
| 00702160 The Great American Country Songbook | $16.99 |
| 00267383 Great American Gospel for Guitar | $12.99 |
| 00702050 Great Classical Themes for Easy Guitar | $8.99 |
| 00702116 Greatest Hymns for Guitar | $10.99 |
| 00275088 The Greatest Showman | $17.99 |
| 00148030 Halloween Guitar Songs | $14.99 |
| 00702273 Irish Songs | $12.99 |
| 00192503 Jazz Classics for Easy Guitar | $14.99 |
| 00702275 Jazz Favorites for Easy Guitar | $15.99 |
| 00702274 Jazz Standards for Easy Guitar | $17.99 |
| 00702162 Jumbo Easy Guitar Songbook | $19.99 |
| 00232285 La La Land | $16.99 |
| 00702258 Legends of Rock | $14.99 |
| 00702189 MTV's 100 Greatest Pop Songs | $24.95 |
| 00702272 1950s Rock | $15.99 |
| 00702271 1960s Rock | $15.99 |
| 00702270 1970s Rock | $16.99 |
| 00702269 1980s Rock | $15.99 |

| | | |
|---|---|---|
| 00702268 1990s Rock | $19.99 |
| 00109725 Once | $14.99 |
| 00702187 Selections from O Brother Where Art Thou? | $19.99 |
| 00702178 100 Songs for Kids | $14.99 |
| 00702515 Pirates of the Caribbean | $16.99 |
| 00702125 Praise and Worship for Guitar | $10.99 |
| 00287930 Songs from *A Star Is Born, The Greatest Showman, La La Land*, and More Movie Musicals | $16.99 |
| 00702285 Southern Rock Hits | $12.99 |
| 00156420 Star Wars Music | $14.99 |
| 00121535 30 Easy Celtic Guitar Solos | $15.99 |
| 00702156 3-Chord Rock | $12.99 |
| 00702220 Today's Country Hits | $12.99 |
| 00244654 Top Hits of 2017 | $14.99 |
| 00283786 Top Hits of 2018 | $14.99 |
| 00702294 Top Worship Hits | $15.99 |
| 00702255 VH1's 100 Greatest Hard Rock Songs | $29.99 |
| 00702175 VH1's 100 Greatest Songs of Rock and Roll | $27.99 |
| 00702253 Wicked | $12.99 |

## ARTIST COLLECTIONS

| | | |
|---|---|---|
| 00702267 AC/DC for Easy Guitar | $15.99 |
| 00702598 Adele for Easy Guitar | $15.99 |
| 00156221 Adele – 25 | $16.99 |
| 00702040 Best of the Allman Brothers | $16.99 |
| 00702865 J.S. Bach for Easy Guitar | $14.99 |
| 00702169 Best of The Beach Boys | $12.99 |
| 00702292 The Beatles — 1 | $19.99 |
| 00125796 Best of Chuck Berry | $15.99 |
| 00702201 The Essential Black Sabbath | $12.95 |
| 00702250 blink-182 — Greatest Hits | $16.99 |
| 02501615 Zac Brown Band — The Foundation | $19.99 |
| 02501621 Zac Brown Band — You Get What You Give | $16.99 |
| 00702043 Best of Johnny Cash | $16.99 |
| 00702090 Eric Clapton's Best | $12.99 |
| 00702086 Eric Clapton — from the Album Unplugged | $15.99 |
| 00702202 The Essential Eric Clapton | $15.99 |
| 00702053 Best of Patsy Cline | $15.99 |
| 00222697 Very Best of Coldplay – 2nd Edition | $14.99 |
| 00702229 The Very Best of Creedence Clearwater Revival | $15.99 |
| 00702145 Best of Jim Croce | $15.99 |
| 00702219 David Crowder*Band Collection | $12.95 |
| 00702278 Crosby, Stills & Nash | $12.99 |
| 14042809 Bob Dylan | $14.99 |
| 00702276 Fleetwood Mac — Easy Guitar Collection | $16.99 |
| 00139462 The Very Best of Grateful Dead | $15.99 |
| 00702136 Best of Merle Haggard | $14.99 |
| 00702227 Jimi Hendrix — Smash Hits | $19.99 |
| 00702288 Best of Hillsong United | $12.99 |
| 00702236 Best of Antonio Carlos Jobim | $15.99 |

| | | |
|---|---|---|
| 00702245 Elton John — Greatest Hits 1970–2002 | $17.99 |
| 00129855 Jack Johnson | $16.99 |
| 00702204 Robert Johnson | $12.99 |
| 00702234 Selections from Toby Keith — 35 Biggest Hits | $12.95 |
| 00702003 Kiss | $16.99 |
| 00110578 Best of Kutless | $12.99 |
| 00702216 Lynyrd Skynyrd | $16.99 |
| 00702182 The Essential Bob Marley | $14.99 |
| 00146081 Maroon 5 | $14.99 |
| 00121925 Bruno Mars – Unorthodox Jukebox | $12.99 |
| 00702248 Paul McCartney — All the Best | $14.99 |
| 00702129 Songs of Sarah McLachlan | $12.95 |
| 00125484 The Best of MercyMe | $12.99 |
| 02501316 Metallica — Death Magnetic | $19.99 |
| 00702209 Steve Miller Band — Young Hearts (Greatest Hits) | $12.95 |
| 00124167 Jason Mraz | $15.99 |
| 00702096 Best of Nirvana | $15.99 |
| 00702211 The Offspring — Greatest Hits | $12.95 |
| 00138026 One Direction | $14.99 |
| 00702030 Best of Roy Orbison | $16.99 |
| 00702144 Best of Ozzy Osbourne | $14.99 |
| 00702279 Tom Petty | $12.99 |
| 00102911 Pink Floyd | $16.99 |
| 00702139 Elvis Country Favorites | $17.99 |
| 00702293 The Very Best of Prince | $16.99 |
| 00699415 Best of Queen for Guitar | $15.99 |
| 00109279 Best of R.E.M. | $14.99 |
| 00702208 Red Hot Chili Peppers — Greatest Hits | $16.99 |
| 00198960 The Rolling Stones | $16.99 |
| 00174793 The Very Best of Santana | $14.99 |
| 00702196 Best of Bob Seger | $15.99 |

| | | |
|---|---|---|
| 00146046 Ed Sheeran | $17.99 |
| 00702252 Frank Sinatra — Nothing But the Best | $17.99 |
| 00702010 Best of Rod Stewart | $16.99 |
| 00702049 Best of George Strait | $14.99 |
| 00702259 Taylor Swift for Easy Guitar | $15.99 |
| 00254499 Taylor Swift – Easy Guitar Anthology | $19.99 |
| 00702260 Taylor Swift — Fearless | $14.99 |
| 00139727 Taylor Swift — 1989 | $17.99 |
| 00115960 Taylor Swift — Red | $16.99 |
| 00253667 Taylor Swift — Reputation | $17.99 |
| 00702290 Taylor Swift — Speak Now | $16.99 |
| 00702223 Chris Tomlin—Arriving | $16.99 |
| 00232849 Chris Tomlin Collection – 2nd Edition | $12.95 |
| 00702226 Chris Tomlin — See the Morning | $12.95 |
| 00148643 Train | $14.99 |
| 00702427 U2 — 18 Singles | $16.99 |
| 00702108 Best of Stevie Ray Vaughan | $16.99 |
| 00279005 The Who | $14.99 |
| 00702123 Best of Hank Williams | $15.99 |
| 00194548 Best of John Williams | $14.99 |
| 00702111 Stevie Wonder — Guitar Collection | $9.95 |
| 00702228 Neil Young — Greatest Hits | $15.99 |
| 00119133 Neil Young — Harvest | $14.99 |

*Prices, contents and availability subject to change without notice.*

Visit Hal Leonard online at **halleonard.com**

0720
306

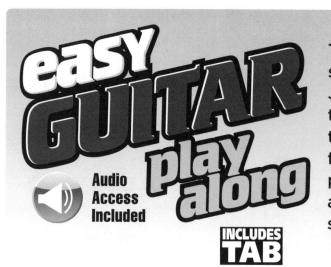

**easy GUITAR play along**

Audio Access Included

INCLUDES TAB

The *Easy Guitar Play Along*® series features streamlined transcriptions of your favorite songs. Just follow the tab, listen to the audio to hear how the guitar should sound, and then play along using the backing tracks. Playback tools are provided for slowing down the tempo without changing pitch and looping challenging parts. The melody and lyrics are included in the book so that you can sing or simply follow along.

## 1. ROCK CLASSICS

Jailbreak • Living After Midnight • Mississippi Queen • Rocks Off • Runnin' Down a Dream • Smoke on the Water • Strutter • Up Around the Bend.

00702560 Book/CD Pack....... $14.99

## 2. ACOUSTIC TOP HITS

About a Girl • I'm Yours • The Lazy Song • The Scientist • 21 Guns • Upside Down • What I Got • Wonderwall.

00702569 Book/CD Pack....... $14.99

## 3. ROCK HITS

All the Small Things • Best of You • Brain Stew (The Godzilla Remix) • Californication • Island in the Sun • Plush • Smells Like Teen Spirit • Use Somebody.

00702570 Book/CD Pack....... $14.99

## 4. ROCK 'N' ROLL

Blue Suede Shoes • I Get Around • I'm a Believer • Jailhouse Rock • Oh, Pretty Woman • Peggy Sue • Runaway • Wake Up Little Susie.

00702572 Book/CD Pack....... $14.99

## 6. CHRISTMAS SONGS

Have Yourself a Merry Little Christmas • A Holly Jolly Christmas • The Little Drummer Boy • Run Rudolph Run • Santa Claus Is Comin' to Town • Silver and Gold • Sleigh Ride • Winter Wonderland.

00101879 Book/CD Pack......... $14.99

## 7. BLUES SONGS FOR BEGINNERS

Come On (Part 1) • Double Trouble • Gangster of Love • I'm Ready • Let Me Love You Baby • Mary Had a Little Lamb • San-Ho-Zay • T-Bone Shuffle.

00103235 Book/
    Online Audio..........$17.99

## 9. ROCK SONGS FOR BEGINNERS

Are You Gonna Be My Girl • Buddy Holly • Everybody Hurts • In Bloom • Otherside • The Rock Show • Santa Monica • When I Come Around.

00103255 Book/CD Pack.....$14.99

## 10. GREEN DAY

Basket Case • Boulevard of Broken Dreams • Good Riddance (Time of Your Life) • Holiday • Longview • 21 Guns • Wake Me up When September Ends • When I Come Around.

00122322 Book/
    Online Audio........$16.99

## 11. NIRVANA

All Apologies • Come As You Are • Heart Shaped Box • Lake of Fire • Lithium • The Man Who Sold the World • Rape Me • Smells Like Teen Spirit.

00122325 Book/
    Online Audio........ $17.99

## 13. AC/DC

Back in Black • Dirty Deeds Done Dirt Cheap • For Those About to Rock (We Salute You) • Hells Bells • Highway to Hell • Rock and Roll Ain't Noise Pollution • T.N.T. • You Shook Me All Night Long.

14042895 Book/
    Online Audio........ $17.99

## 14. JIMI HENDRIX – SMASH HITS

All Along the Watchtower • Can You See Me • Crosstown Traffic • Fire • Foxey Lady • Hey Joe • Manic Depression • Purple Haze • Red House • Remember • Stone Free • The Wind Cries Mary.

00130591 Book/
    Online Audio........$24.99

**HAL•LEONARD®**

**www.halleonard.com**

Prices, contents, and availability subject to change without notice.